MISHA
USOV

HOW TO
NOT BE AFRAID
OF BEING
YOURSELF

ARTISTE
CIRQUE DU SOLEIL

THE
INVISIBLE
CLOWN

THE INVISIBLE
CLOWN

How to not be afraid of
BEING YOURSELF

by Misha Usov
Artiste
Cirque du Soleil

Published by Misha Usov

Copyright © 2021 Misha Usov

Photographs: Dirk Weyer, Photography + Motion
Illustrations in the book: Ángel Idígoras
Illustrations on the back cover: Vladimir Zimakov
Translation: Kevin Bridge
Book Production: Margaret Campbell

This book is set in Book Antiqua
Printed in the United States of America

First Edition: October 2021

ISBN: 9798524733825

There are three types of actors: bad actors,
good actors, and great actors.
Everything is clear with the bad ones,
their acting is mediocre, the good ones — play good.
The great actors do not play anything at all —
they just live in front of the camera.

- Alain Delon

In the theatre of human life the role of the onlookers
is reserved only for God and the angels.

- Francis Bacon

DEDICATION

For all the students in the world.
And for all the teachers,
who also continue to learn.

CONTENTS

INTRODUCTION

Every one of us sooner or later wonders: *Who am I? How can I be myself? What is my calling? How can I be happy?*

In childhood we do not encounter these questions, we are happy because we are ourselves.

As we become adults, however, new psychological processes are activated internally and we start to acquire templates — these templates arise from our upbringing, education, and our perception of the world. These templates become bad habits and develop into fears, into a lack of self-confidence, or into arrogance and even cynicism. These traits actually block us from accessing who we truly are.

When I was developing the idea for this book I just wanted to write about stage fright and how to combat it. But now the book is finished — and I have come to learn that it is about how to be happy. If you like, it's my clown's recipe for happiness, my vitamin D for my dear readers.

This book will be useful to anyone who wants to find themselves and how to be themselves, and anyone who has to speak in public: to play a role, stand in front of a video or stills camera, read a report, perform auditions, and present their projects. It is based on my own practical experience. The majority of books that are available now on public performance or self-development, yoga, meditation and so on, offer the reader a range of techniques.

More often than not these books teach you how to speak beautifully, how to move correctly, and how to meditate. There is merit, however, in plunging into everyday life — stopping by the baker for a loaf of 'Borodinskiy,' going into your boss's office, or climbing onto the podium to make a speech as a leader — any negative look, or word, directed at you from the sales assistant, from your boss, a friend, or from anyone else, activates psychological mechanisms. These are dependent on your upbringing and your education, and were formed back then when you had not yet tested 'what is right and wrong' on yourself, when you were simply told something and you believed it. Since we, as a rule, are not self-aware we simply copy models of behaviour from others. This is how these psychological mechanisms begin to work inside of us, and we, since we are not self-aware, begin to perceive the world anew according to templates. We lose confidence in ourselves and our self-worth diminishes, or we go the other way and become excessively arrogant.

By not finding your true self, you want to be like your teacher, friend, boss, or a famous artist or sports figure — but in doing so you will be living someone else's life.

With the development of technology we emigrate to social media, but even there we do not feel happy since it depends on the number of likes and subscribers and on the opinions of others.

It does not matter whether we are on stage, in everyday life, or online. How can we be ourselves? How can we be happy? How can we avoid being dependent on the reactions of others? How can we avoid experiencing stress before and during a speech in front of a large or small audience? How can we not be afraid of the video or still camera? How can we not be nervous of interviews, business meetings, auditions, or work meetings? How can we gain charisma?

These days we have to appear in front of the public almost all the time in some way or other: either on stage, as we are recording our vlogs, attending online courses, auditions, webinars, commenting on events, or giving and conducting interviews.

In this book I share my own experience as a circus clown and explain how I have interacted with audiences on all five continents of our unbelievable planet over the course of 36 years. On stage I do not say a word — and this book is testimony to what I am silent about.

The book describes real events from my artistic life, which have helped me find myself. I have intentionally changed the names of the heroes of the book because firstly, their prototypes are people who are alive and well in the present day and I do not want to offend them, or for them to beat me up in some back street. Secondly, when I looked at the draft that used their real names it seemed boring and mundane to me.

Who is this book for? It is for my 20-year-old self. The naïve, self-doubting, audacious, artistic, self-willed, stubborn, unbelievably proud and vain young man with low self-esteem, who did not pass a single audition. It is also for my 30-year-old self, who knew his first taste of success and was afraid of losing it. It is also for my 40-year-old self, a man who had lost his youth and was emulating anyone who was cooler, funnier, wiser, and who wanted to relive his younger years but in a more conscious way. This book is for anyone who wants to get back to who they are, and also for anyone who just wants to spend their time being happy.

Observing today's young people I notice that they differ only slightly from my 20-year-old self. Although back then I did not have a smartphone and all the new technology, a computer and so on, I am similar to them, especially when it comes to my internal manifestations.

Dear reader, what you are going to discover in this book will help you not only on stage, but also in REAL LIFE.

- Misha

Part One

TIMING

CHAPTER 1

The Time of The Invisible Clown

*On how easy it is to lose yourself
and where to look for yourself afterwards*

One day, two groups of children were brought to our circus: one group were boys and girls of around seven or eight years of age, while the others were nine or ten years of age. I, as a clown, was asked to conduct a master class with them. I worked with each group separately at different times.

I asked both groups to do exactly the same exercise: to choose a part of the body to lead and move forward. That is to say, one specific part of their body should be the most prominent, and drag the rest along behind so to speak. As an example, I demonstrated to the children how my stomach could 'lead', and how it could take the rest of my body along with it. I asked the children to come up with their own variant for this exercise. The children in the first group were absorbed in creativity, inventing their own interpretations.

One little girl put her elbow out in front of her, and her elbow gave her direction. Another child let his index finger lead the rest of his body. It looked really funny. Another boy lay on the floor and started to crawl like a caterpillar, demonstrating that it was his head that led the rest of his body. The children were prepared to make fantasies and create their own interpretations.

It was hard for the slightly older children from the second group to find their own movement, they were reserved and almost all of them copied me, demonstrating how big their stomachs were.

They did not look for their own variant. The impression was that the children did not want to stand out. They wanted to be like everyone else. It appears that in terms of the development of a child's personality — this is normal. How though can we avoid being trapped at this level?

This small example demonstrates how we lose our individuality at a sufficiently young age, when we want to be like adults and we accumulate templates. Children of seven years of age, however, are still free to express themselves.

There are just a few fortunate individuals, who are less prone to this bad habit of thinking and acting in terms of templates, and we perceive them almost as heroes, those we would like to emulate.

I will tell you about the method I use to look for and find myself, to be myself, and to be happy.

This book consists of three parts: 'Timing,' 'Character,' and 'State,' in which I examine in detail each of the most important components of my methodology. The 11 lessons, one of which I was taught by my second teacher, the King of the Absurd, and 12 exercises, will help you assimilate new skills and put them into practice. So that you can rest a little, and can smile and be inspired, I will also tell you in three chapters about my three teachers — about the King of Fate, the King of the Absurd, and the King of Hearts.

As I am a professional clown, I wanted to lift the lid behind the scenes of my surprising profession, and demonstrate, through a clown's view of life, how to be happy.

A CLOWN IS A RARE PROFESSION

A very famous clown once told me how one young girl had decided to commit suicide, but she did not go through with it because, completely by chance, she had been to the circus and had watched his show.

Although I have never brought anyone back from suicide, I do receive, with sufficient regularity, comments on my posts and clowning videos on social media. People write about how these videos help them out of depression. For example, I received this feedback:

*'A wonderful show, it makes me sad when I am happy,
and happy when I am sad.'*

When we toured Canada with our show, people would come up to the staff entrance of the circus and ask me to give master-classes — not about clowning, however, but about how to be happy. They were hoping that clowns knew a secret of some kind to happiness.

This reminded me of an incident that happened to me and my friend, and first clowning partner, Knyaz Melik Ter-Compassion. (As I mentioned above, this is a made-up name, as, incidentally, are many of the names in this book, although the heroes and the stories are true). Anyway, my friend and

I, a wonderful contemporary clown, whom many of you, if I were to reveal his real name, would know well, traveled with a touring group around Kazakhstan right at the start of our artistic careers back in the Soviet Union.

After the shows a queue of sick children with their parents lined up to see us — a number of them were in wheelchairs, and some were on crutches. They believed that we, as clowns, who were then both 16 years old, could heal them. In certain areas in Central Asia a clown is a holy figure, not unlike a cow in India or a holy fool in old Russia.

My partner Knyaz, who is Armenian but actually from Azerbaijan, was not puzzled by any of this, and he began to 'heal' these unfortunate children. He told me to get a few newspapers and burn them in an aluminum basin. This is what I did.

We set ourselves up on the stage, having lined the children up in a queue. I held the basin with the ashes. Knyaz, muttering something in Armenian, sprinkled those ashes on the heads of the unfortunate children. As a token of their gratitude, the parents showered us with food — eggs, milk, onions, potatoes, noodles, and kumis.

I do not know if the children were cured or not, but at least, seeing the suffering of the children and their parents, we tried not to destroy their hope and their faith in a miracle.

Those suggestions in Canada, the comments on my videos, as well as the personal messages from both young people and those who are not so young, engendered in me a desire to share my knowledge and to help people overcome their insecurity, their fears, and help them get back to who they are. The sense of this was more or less the same — a request to learn how not to take life so seriously. I also wanted to let the reader know about my master classes, which every now and again I conduct worldwide.

If back then in Kazakhstan we naively sprinkled ashes on the heads of the sick children in an attempt to give them and their parents even the smallest hope, then now my experience, which I have gained as a result of my search, can really help others.

A clown is the most benign, and the scarcest profession in the world. As we say in the circus: 'Look after the clowns. There are fewer real clowns than there are cosmonauts.'

Anatoliy Marchevskiy, a famous Soviet clown, director of the Yekaterinburg circus and founder of the World Festival of Clowns in Yekaterinburg, said that since he needed to invite real professionals to the festival every year, he and his team counted the number of clowns around the world, and it turned out there were approximately 200 on the entire planet.

Imagine that, today there are a little less than eight billion people living on Earth, and only approximately 200 of them are real clowns.

Kindness cannot be performed, you have to have it somewhere deep inside you. If you were to say evil clowns do exist, then I would answer you saying: they are not clowns at all, they are imitations.

'Why?' — some readers may ask.

Because all of the real clowns — and there are very few of them — are my friends. Believe me, I have not seen anyone evil among those 200 people. A bad person would not take up this profession, because they could not be sincerely funny, and are more likely to be aggressive. The public would not accept a clown like that. Who then would invite a clown like that to work for them?

It's a paradox, but given such a small number of real clowns they are all but unheard of. They are also rarely seen at the cinema or on television. Sometimes, older clowns are shown around Christmas time, without a doubt they are the legendary clowns:

Charlie Chaplin, Grock, Joe Jackson, Charlie Rivel, Nikulin, Shuydin, Karandash, and Laurel and Hardy among others.

Why though were they famous back then? Why are they still famous even now?

Recently I went into an Irish bar in Frankfurt. Behind the bar, in black bowler hats and wearing wry grins, were Laurel and Hardy — or to be more precise their sculptures made of wood.

Maybe they became famous against the backdrop of the universal turmoil at the time of the Great Depression, world war, and post-war hardship. Perhaps these great clowns were sent to Earth to give people a little hope.

Then again, a clown's boots can now be purchased in an ordinary shoe shop, and the more expensive the boots, the closer they resemble a clown's boots. The same goes for clothes. Chequered clothes made in different shapes, ornately decorated by contemporary designers, funny hats, loud socks and shorts, and jackets turned inside out. Is that not a clown's attire?

Another paradox is that the word 'clown' can sometimes take on a negative connotation. For example, if you do something silly you will, sooner or later, be dubbed: 'clown!' This is how some politicians are called clowns.

In America, following the Tommy Lee Wallis film 'It' (1990), which was based on the Stephen King novel of the same name, people began to be really afraid of clowns. One film changes the perception of this kind-hearted and rare profession across a huge country, despite the fact that the hero was only evil in the mind of the director.

In the USA even today, coulrophobia continues. The second film recently came out, 'It Chapter Two,' after which my eldest daughter said:

'Dad, do you eat children or something?'

'My dear daughter, what made you ask that?'

'At school one of my classmates said: "So your dad is a clown — that means he eats children." I proved to them that you were a good person, but after that film they began to be afraid of you.'

WHAT DO YOU DO?

Overall, I personally have always held a positive attitude about myself and my profession. When people ask me what I do for a living, I usually respond by saying: 'I'm a clown.' I've noticed that people become children again for a short time on hearing just that one word in response. A broad smile appears on some people's faces and their eyes light up. There are instances however, when the opposite happens.

One elderly lady, when I told her that I was a clown, asked me to make her laugh. I poked my tongue out at her — like Albert Einstein.

As far as I could tell she did not understand. Everyone around her laughed but she stood there looking at me for a long time, just like this:

It seems to me that Albert Einstein was also a clown. On his 72nd birthday he poked his tongue out at reporters who time and again asked him to smile for the camera. Is that not a clown's approach to this request?

On another occasion we were dining with friends in New York in a French restaurant, and a trustworthy man from the Italian embassy, who looked to be 60 years of age, asked me to demonstrate to him what a clown was. At that moment he was about to put a piece of steak into his mouth. I took hold of his left hand and changed the direction of movement of that piece of steak. Instead of going into the Italian's open mouth I put the steak instead in his neighbour's mouth, who had been playing along with me.

Why are people fascinated with clowns? It is clowns who break the molds, destroy the prevailing order. This profession enables an adult to remain a child. My eldest daughter, when she was six, said to me that she did not want to grow up, the adult world just held no attraction for her.

Maybe this is because people are not kind-hearted enough? People are very serious with one another and with those around them. We have learned to socialize freely on the Internet, but when it comes to face-to-face meetings, it turns out that this is not so easy.

In any group of people you can almost always find someone who likes to crack jokes. Without knowing it they immediately unite a group of people, and everyone around becomes a little happier. A good joke defuses an atmosphere of mistrust and brings people closer.

Politicians and businessmen sometimes use humour at difficult times during intense negotiations, in order to defuse an emotionally charged atmosphere. I know one businessman who deliberately brought along a professional clown to some important business meetings. At first glance the clown looked just like him, both dressed in suit and tie. As soon as any difficulties arose, however, he would pull a funny trick using sleight of hand or would sometimes just sit down without saying a word, and his presence alone would bring relief.

People want to love and to be loved and they want to be happy. Humour is one of the key things on the path to this. In my opinion, this is the reason why I come across a desire among such completely diverse groups of people to get to know the profession of a clown better. Some of them even request clowning master-classes tailored to them.

A clown is a very rare profession, but a teacher of this profession is even more rare. To find such a teacher is a great achievement.

It seems to me that one of these clown master-classes can take the place of several trips to a psychologist. It will help you rise above yourself, to look at yourself from a different perspective, and as a result to see your INVISIBLE self. The side of you that is invisible to the public who will no longer see you as you are with all your worries, cares and strivings.Instead they will see your inexplicable energy, your charisma, the magic of your performance, and the light that you are projecting. They will not be able to take their eyes off of you.

Reflecting from this perspective on how to become happier, and on how to not be afraid of performing in front of the public, you will be able to open up something new within yourself, something unknown.

9

IN SEARCH OF A METHOD

When I was 20 years of age, my friend and first clowning partner, Knyaz Melik Ter-Compassion, said that he wanted to find the secret to being funny and charismatic, independent of any circumstances.

'Should it not be that way,' he said, 'should all the kings of comedy not know how to be funny whenever they want?'

More than thirty years have passed since that moment. That question has tormented me as well. I have put this question to many famous clowns, artistes, and directors. After studying at the professional clowning studio for five years, I learned many funny tricks. I, however, still could not find an answer. The more I worked as a professional clown, the more acute this question became. The public would laugh to their heart's content at one joke on one day, and you would be besieged by fans, the press would be calling you the next Charlie Chaplin. But the next day that same joke would not work at all, the fans would turn away and professionals would call you a 'weak clown.'

When you are on stage in front of the public anything can happen. Sometimes in the auditorium at the most inopportune moment a baby would start crying loudly, or the lighting technician would forget to shine the light onto you, or just as you are about to go on stage you are asked: 'Are you going to be dining after the show? Should we book you a table?'

Or someone tries to bring down your self worth, for example by saying: 'I saw such and such a clown, and he was really funny…' Then you immediately understand that what this person wanted to say is that you are not funny enough. You retreat into your own thoughts and your self-worth diminishes. It is in this state of mind that you have to go on stage — and make people laugh. The magic of the performance in the end is destroyed, and the success and career of a clown goes down with it.

On average, circus artistes might perform up to 40 shows per month.

How can clowns be funny almost every day? How do they remain true to themselves performing in front of a small or large auditorium? Why do they not fear the public?

How do they remain independent of internal and external circumstances? Why do they not experience stress?

These questions really worried me a great deal, and I could not find answers to them anywhere. So I decided to unlock the secret to success myself, based on my own experience.

The first thing I did was to study the life and work of clowns, both famous and not so famous. The answer, however, did not reveal itself. On the contrary, even more questions arose.

Then I decided to look at things from the other way round and studied the biographies of famous tragic actors, but here too I could not latch on to anything. To play a dramatic role they recalled their saddest moments in life and, with the help of these memories, they could convey sadness and could even make themselves, and the audience, cry. Considering we play around nine or ten shows a week you can imagine what would happen if I, in my desire to make people laugh, recalled one and the same joke, and the funniest thing that happened to me in life, every day, and sometimes several times a day. One and the same joke told every day, several times a day, would stop being funny, at least for the one telling it.

When I asked myself what was stopping me from being a good clown, the answer was 'Stage fright. A fear of failure.'

Fears were destroying me, and they were also destroying

the magic of my performance. It seemed to me that I was an unconvincing clown, it seemed like nobody believed me, and therefore nobody laughed. It seemed like an enormous image of Stanislavskiy's face in his round glasses was following me everywhere. As I stepped onto the stage the image of his face would instantly say:

I DON'T BELIEVE YOU!

These words would hit me hard between the eyes and would kill any hope that at some point Konstantin Sergeyevich would say:

I believe you!

For the most part this happened at critical moments, such as when my act was being recorded for television. Or when another very famous clown was sitting in the auditorium. Or when a foreign impresario would come to invite me to work for him on an important contract. And so on. Therefore I dreamed of finding a method so that the fears no longer troubled me. They would no longer destroy me in front of the public.

I noticed that I was much funnier when I was physically tired, such as after a long-haul flight or a 12-hour drive and I was due to go on stage that same day. The fears would disappear as a result of my tiredness, I did not act anything out, I just wanted one thing — to finish my performance as soon as possible and go to the hotel to rest. It was as though my mind was also exhausted and did not interfere in the performance process. As a rule, the charisma showed through on those days and the public was very accepting of me.

Clearly, my fears arose out of a desire to please the public and it was this desire that was stopping me from being funny. When I was exhausted, however, I would not even be thinking about what the public might like, or not like.

I continued my search. Sometimes it seemed to me that it was not me who was trying to find out how not to be afraid of the public and how to be funny, and these same questions continued to search for answers independent of me.

MY MOSCOW EXPERIENCE

On one occasion, when I was still studying clowning in Moscow, I needed to perform with my friend Knyaz at a stadium in the Podmoskovye region. We were due to perform the act known as the 'Apple.'

During the course of my study of clowning in the studio I had completely lost my sense of the comic. There was a great deal of theory in our clowning classes, but much less practical learning about performing in front of the public. Before we started studying in the studio, Knyaz and I had performed this act many times, but unfortunately around this time it had been completely unsuccessful.

We would read the script mechanically and receive

stereotypical responses — we had failed in our own performance yet again. At that time it happened so often and was so distressing that I wanted to change my profession.

The fear of another failure, and my lack of belief in myself were poisoning my existence. The closer the performance came the worse I would sleep at night. This would happen especially towards morning, when I was completely vulnerable and my mind would conjure up unsettling images of failure on stage.

In the evening the day before the performance, I was on my way back from the Usachyovskiy baths in Moscow. On the way home I briefly went to the Usachyovskiy market and purchased a single apple for our act. I decided to rehearse a little one more time. I lifted the apple up to my eye level, and suddenly I heard a clear voice in my head say: 'Look at the apple!'

I looked at the apple and I saw thousands of individual details, its bright red colour fading to a burgundy red against the grey, autumnal Moscow skies. I saw hundreds of fractures, dark spots, wormholes, and flashes from the city lights. I saw the apple for the first time. These insignificant details awakened distinct, inexplicable emotions in my consciousness. I was engulfed by gentleness, goodness, and a light melancholy, which blended in with the autumnal sorrow.

Maybe I had experienced this emotion before in my childhood. When I was eight years old, I had ridden into a swarm of midges on my bicycle, and I had enjoyed it so much that I decided to feed myself to each of these midges. 'Eat me midges! Eat me!' I shouted to them.

It is really difficult to describe that state of being. You are filled with a unfounded joy, with gratitude, you become very small in comparison to this feeling, which, like an ocean wave, comes over you and engulfs you from head to toe, and what is more, you see, hear, and empathize.

The text of the clowning act the 'Apple' had been creeping up on me, but I could not yet voice it. At that point it would have been false.

Despite the fact that the next day I had to go on stage, thanks to the state of being that had engulfed me on the way home from the Usachyovskiy baths I began to feel good and my mood was relaxed. I fell asleep quickly and slept very well. I did not have any nightmares and all my fears had scattered.

The next day, on the morning of the day the show was to take place, I tried again to rehearse this act. I looked at the apple with the same look as I had done the evening before — and it had the same effect. The previous day's sensations spread fondly throughout my body. I could not understand this at all: what else did I need to rehearse?

That evening I went on stage in this wonderful state of being. I did next to nothing, just occasionally looked at the apple. The public laughed their heads off. It was unbelievably successful, even though I had not said a word. Knyaz voiced the text of this clowning act for himself, and for me.

I was so happy that even today I remember almost every tree outside the window that we passed on the road into Moscow. I remember the other artistes on that bus and the feeling of unity with each of them. Knyaz said to me: 'I don't know what happened to you, why you said nothing. But it was really funny. The public loved us so much they are asking us to perform this act here every week on Fridays and Saturdays.'

At a lesson in the clowning studio the following day I performed a small observational sketch: A man is reading the paper, but actually he is covered in this paper so he can eat the apple without being seen; but he cannot eat it, and he just looks at it. After doing this sketch, I remained in that state of being.

My clowning teacher, whom we will discuss more in the

second part of the book, immediately noticed the changes in me. He told me: 'Remember that! That's your charisma — the organic nature of a clown.'

Having committed this experience to memory I understood the direction I needed to go in my search. I had to create a special state of being within myself, which I later called: THE INVISIBLE CLOWN.

THE JOKER AND THE FOUR SUITS: WHAT AN INVISIBLE CLOWN IS

I came up with the concept of the Invisible Clown after I read the book *Human Types* by Susan Zannos[1], in which, with the help of a conventional pack of playing cards, the author explains the apparatus of the human psyche. As the author confirms, the tradition of correlating our psychology with these cards originated quite some time ago.

I do not know in which period in history, or why, people began to see in the cards symbols of the manifestation of our psychological nature. But when I began to observe myself, and others, from this same point of view, I discovered that I was dealing with an inspired approach. It not only helped me with clowning, in building my acts and shows, but also in everyday life. Thanks to these cards I began to understand myself better and accept myself and those around me. Furthermore, I had not found anything like this in any other books on the art of performing. Therefore, I suggest just trying out this theory.

In order to explain what an 'invisible clown' means, we will need a standard French deck of playing cards — 54 cards in total: 52 main cards and two special cards: the so-called jokers.

[1] Zannos, S. Human Types. Building the Body and Psychology. – M.: IG 'Ves', 2003

16

The words 'joker', 'fool', 'jester', 'comic', or 'clown' in essence mean the same thing. For me, a clown is a joker in his highest manifestation.

On playing cards the whole of the joker is shown, that is to say the whole body, whereas with the kings, queens and jacks only the top half of the body is shown.

The joker, in contrast to the kings, queens, and jacks, holds all the suits in his hand — and according to ancient beliefs these suits correspond to four human characteristics. The clubs relate to instinct; the spades — to movement; the hearts — to emotions; the diamonds — to intellect. Therefore, the joker holds in his hands his emotions, his intellect, his movements, and his instincts.

I called the joker an Invisible Clown since his elevated experiences are invisible to the naked eye. Whatever you say about the kings, queens and jacks — the manifestations of their characters are visible to us. For example, when I, along with my circus clique, go to the circus as part of the audience, we make a point of applauding the artistes for their small tricks, which a casual observer would not even notice. There is a reason behind our bursting into applause though, because the the public would join in. This activates the card of the jack.

The jacks are soldiers: they do what they are told, without thinking. In the 1990s in Moscow at the time of food shortages enormous queues formed for all manner of things. We recorded a few jokes for a candid camera comedy television programme. There were six of us in all, and we were dressed in everyday clothes. One of us would turn to face a brick wall. Another clown would form up behind him, behind this second clown a third, and so on, until a queue of six people was formed. Five minutes later a queue of 50 people were standing behind us. Only after ten minutes did people begin to ask: why are we standing here?

17

Another time, we bought a sewing pattern to sew an ordinary dress, and pretended it was a map of Moscow we showed it to people on the street, asking them: how do we get to Yakimanka Street? The majority of people, even without thinking, showed us the way to Yakimanka on the sewing pattern. This is how the jack works: without thinking, that is to say subconsciously.

The queens are more attentive, but they experience extreme emotions. An individual may really like something one minute, and a minute later hate it.

In *Alice in Wonderland* Lewis Carroll reveals the image of the queen, who orders her people to chop off everyone's heads left and right, while the king is pardoning everybody.

The king has more attentive and noble qualities. He is able to see what other people need and are able to assess a situation more accurately. That is why when we are standing on stage, it is useful for us to possess the qualities of a king.

The kings still want to lead people to the Invisible Clown and are able to so, but they can never be the Invisible Clown or the joker.

There are two jokers. The author of the book *Human Types* tells us that one of these jokers represents our HIGHER EMOTIONS while the other represents our HIGHER INTELLECT.

In our case — these are the Invisible Clown and the Great Viewer.

So, dear reader, now that you are familiar with the idea that the cards symbolize the manifestation of our psyche, and you have learned the unique characteristics of the joker, you can understand what the Invisible Clown actually is.

The state of the Invisible Clown is one in which we experience higher emotions. These experiences are linked to the here and now. On a psychological level we transcend the boundaries of time and for us the only thing that exists is the 'Now'. There is no primary reason for this, it exists in us of itself. The more we practice the state of the Invisible Clown, the more this feeling grows deeper and brighter. Like mountains or an ocean: no matter how long we look at them, they are always changing. It's impossible to grow tired of them. Therefore, the state of the Invisible Clown never repeats itself: with each moment it develops new characteristics, and we never grow tired of it. In addition, apart from the state of the Invisible Clown is a state of empathy, real unconditional love, which we experience on its own implicit terms.

IN SEARCH OF THE STATE OF THE INVISIBLE CLOWN

I received several answers to my questions — but I encountered difficulties. I discovered that I was not able to experience the state of the Invisible Clown at will.

The state arose completely by chance and by no means at every show. I began to study the nature of this state. No matter where my searches led me, however, it seemed much further away than I had anticipated, and it was much bigger than clowning itself. In simple, day-to-day life this answer helped me more than once; not only did it help me: I saw that without it my life was a biological existence, or an existence within the prison of my own illusions.

At that time there was no Google, and I could not find any of the information I needed. Then I went to the bookshop on the Noviy Arbat in Moscow, looking for books on performing. There were sufficient numbers of books on sale on this topic, but I understood that I would not find the answers there. The books discussed different acting techniques. I already knew all of these techniques. We were taught them over the course of four years in the clowning studio. Completely by chance, I stumbled upon a book in the shop called *In Search of the Miraculous* by Pyotr Ouspensky, but, on opening the book on a page with a multitude of geometric diagrams, I put it back on the shelf. In the evening of that day I told my friend about my trip to the bookshop. He is the wonderful Cream Clown who is known throughout the former Soviet Union, and someone I trusted completely. After smoking his cigarette he pulled out of his rucksack that same book *In Search of the Miraculous* by Pyotr Ouspensky: 'This should help you.'

Pyotr Demyanovich Ouspensky's *In Search of the Miraculous*, an author and philosopher who lived in the first half of the 20th century, was a student of the famous mystic Georgiy Ivanovich Gurdzhiev, a legendary figure. Ouspensky's book has changed the lives of many people. Much later I read an interview with the famous American clown Jango Edwards. The journalist asked Jango how he became a clown, and he answered: 'I became a clown after I had read Pyotr Ouspensky's book *In Search of the Miraculous*.'

To say that this book astonished me would be to say nothing. A description of my impressions of this book would fill a whole other book. I read Ouspensky over three summer months and it was from his work that I learned how to look for that particular state of consciousness: with the help of religion and art. The aim of any true religion and the aim of true, objective art is to convey this state, since it is this that makes it possible to connect with the Divine.

I learned that there is objective and subjective art, and that this state can never be attained from subjective art. It can only be acquired through objective art. So, I began to look for signs of this state in different art forms. I saw that true art really does convey it: 'The St Matthew Passion,' by Johann Sebastian Bach is able to induce this state from the very first notes.

It was then, when I was reading this book in my flat on Shabolovka in Moscow. In the kitchen at night, when everyone else was asleep, I put on my headphones, sat in the lotus position on an ancient leather sofa, and switched on 'The St Matthew Passion'…In the silence the candle flickered on the kitchen table. From the very first notes my eyes closed, my breath quickened, and suddenly an unbelievable force of some kind began to spin me around inside itself. It was as though I had entered a centrifuge. I was spinning so much that it seemed like I was about to go outside of myself, while my body remained sitting on the sofa. I was preparing to have an out-of-body experience, like a cosmonaut who performs a space walk. I was getting ready to enter eternity. It seemed so real and so natural that I became frightened and stopped the experiment, tearing off the headphones sharply.

Artists can also convey this experience. Fra Angelico, for example, decorated the walls of many of the buildings at the San Marco friary in Florence with scenes from the New Testament. If you stand for long enough before his frescoes you will definitely experience this state.

Or the 'Return of the Prodigal Son' by Rembrandt. You can see how carefully the naked heel under the sandal that has been torn off the prodigal son's foot is painted, and you understand how long it took the artist to paint this, and how much oil went into painting just that heel. This is to convey to us the idea of how much the prodigal son had to suffer, how many roads he had to walk, on his way back to his father, who humbly and submissively hugs his prodigal child. The entire composition induces humility, and along with it — that wonderful state of consciousness.

The pyramids of Egypt, the Great Sphinx, Notre-Dame Cathedral in Paris, Chartres Cathedral, the Church of the Intercession on the Nerl, the work of the ancient Greek sculptors — all these works of art convey this same state, that of the Invisible Clown.

I recently spent some time at the Doge's Palace in Venice. Just 30 steps from this wonderful building once stood a terrible prison that did not have any windows. A small bridge linked this building with the palace. The prisoners lived next to the most beautiful structure in Europe, full of treasures and light, with huge windows that looked out onto San Marino and the lagoon. The prisoners had no access to the palace, with the exception of when they were taken over the bridge to be put on trial and brought back again.

We are in the same situation as those prisoners. Our situation is even more dramatic, because the fortresses, guards and even the sentence itself are our own illusions. There are no fortresses, no guards, and the bridge is always open. The pleasures of the palace table are ready! All we have to do is to leave our own nauseating cells, climb up onto the bridge, and enter the palace.

How can we open that door that has no locks? How can we wake up and discover that our crimes, and even the sentence itself, are nothing but a dream?

CHAPTER 2

Where Do Invisible Clowns Live and How Can We Meet Them?

In the first chapter we learned that we perceive the world through templates. These templates open the door to fears and close us off from our true selves. It is because of these templates that we are living someone else's life. Unsatisfied with our own lives we suppose that happiness, which nature provides for everyone, is slipping away from us.

We also learned that our fears arise out of our desire for success, our desire to please people or please the public. We are afraid that we will not be successful.

Using my clowning experience as an example we saw that fears can be countered with the help of the state of the Invisible Clown.

In this chapter let's prepare for a journey to visit an Invisible Clown.

FREEDOM OF CHOICE

Every human being is born with freedom of choice, but we do not make use of it — more often than not, we imitate this choice, living someone else's life in accordance with a template.

This happens because we do not know ourselves. The more an individual recognizes their true selves the more they distance themselves from anything they do not see as their identity, even their name. Freedom of choice is born of whatever is left. In this sense the assertion, 'Man is the architect of his happiness,' is relevant.

Whatever an individual wants they will obtain sooner or later. This is evident in the example of our incomes. I noticed that the bigger my dream is, the more money I have in the bank. Someone has a dream of buying a new television and they will of course buy it, but they will spend all their money on it. Someone else dreams of purchasing their own home and they will achieve it without fail.

I am afraid that many readers will object. They will say: 'It is better not to provide any evidence at all if it can't be supported in fact.'

Dear reader, I have tested this on myself. Just believe me, it works. Moreover, my friend, a famous acrobat told me about this phenomenon a long time ago. He has won gold medals at all the most prestigious circus competitions around the world. He thinks that real love can only be unconditional. Therefore let's name him here Mr. Unconditional.

The absurdity of the situation is that we save money so that we will have more of it. But the amount of money we get is exactly equal to what we need, or to how big the scale of our dream is.

This same law works in the field of stage performance as well. If you want to give lectures, think in terms of a whole cycle of lectures. If you want to prepare a new act — then think about a show. If you want to have your own show — start dreaming about your own repertory theatre. You always have to take one step forward in everything. All it takes is one step to surpass yourself a little.

PREPARING FOR THE JOURNEY

There is no need to pack your suitcases, as we would normally do ahead of setting off on a journey to visit an Invisible Clown. On the contrary, we should start by unpacking these suitcases — everything is topsy-turvy for a clown.

We need to unpack everything from the suitcase, not forgetting a thing, and then carefully fold away everything in its place in the cupboard or on a shelf, socks go with socks, shirts go with shirts…

The suitcases themselves can be put in the storeroom. It is important to fold these items away carefully because we are going to need their names, and the names of the shelves on which they sit.

All these items are our masks, which we put on as we do an item of clothing, when we meet people in various situations, and specifically, when we stand on stage in front of the public.

This clothing that we need to leave in the wardrobe represents our illusory perception of our own selves, as well as being an illusory picture of how everything should be.

They represent our fears, our desire to dominate.

This is our greed, especially at those moments when we are standing on stage with all our partners, or with a partner.

We want the public to love us alone, and therefore we are not prepared to share.

This is our manipulation of people. Often this takes the form of us engaging in intellectual conversations in order to obtain something, or to appear more intelligent.

Our own self-will, our decision not to submit to the will of the director, or of our boss — this represents us saying 'NO' deep inside, even if we do not show this.

Our non-existence is our desire to waste our time on frivolous pursuits.

Our naivete is our lack of willingness to learn from our own mistakes, or those of others.

Our suitcases are what these 'items of clothing' are packed in. This is our striving to behave well, not to lift our head above the parapet but be like everyone else, or on the other hand, not to be like everyone else. More often than not this suitcase is called a vanity suitcase. All the items of clothing are merely its attributes.

When we leave all the items of clothing and the suitcase in their place, we begin our journey to the Invisible Clown. This also means being sincere. It means appearing in front of the public fully clothed — but feeling completely naked, unprotected in a psychological sense.

The Invisible Clown lives inside anyone who performs on stage, and furthermore, the Invisible Clown lives in each one of us, even if we are not aware of it.

The Invisible Clown is the most generous, most modest, and the most unrestrained. The Invisible Clown holds everything back, and yet holds nothing back.

ADAM — THE FIRST INVISIBLE CLOWN

It seems to me that Invisible Clowns have always lived, since the dawn of time. Moreover, Adam, the first human on earth, was an Invisible Clown. It would be curious to observe Adam's reactions immediately after he appeared on earth. After all, he knew nothing at that point. It is possible that our Invisible Clown lives in this state. It is hidden away deep inside of us. Is it completely hidden though?

When you succeed in journeying within yourself and you reach your Invisible Clown, you will understand that he is not your own *personal* clown. What is more striking is that the Invisible Clown is here FOREVER, while you are not.

When I first joined Cirque du Soleil, I was taught how to apply make-up professionally, and I spent an hour and a half on it. Seven years later and this now takes me 20 minutes. As I discovered, however, it would take me an entire lifetime to find my Invisible Clown, and possibly, not just one lifetime...

My third teacher, the King of Hearts, once said to me:

'In order to understand what love is,
you have to understand what antipathy is.'

Let's try to use this observation and research what an Invisible Clown is, and what he is not.

At the same time we will find out who is able to see an Invisible Clown, and who cannot.

In our search we will rely on 11 Rules, which I will discuss over the entire course of the book. Anyone who observes these rules can entertain the hope of succeeding in recognizing the Invisible Clown inside of them.

RULE 1

**Don't grow a beard to appear more intelligent
and don't put on a red nose to become a clown.
Find that red nose inside of yourself.**

We are not self aware, and therefore we are not familiar with our own personality as we are standing on stage. Externally they, of course, look just like us, but what emotions are they going through inside, especially when they are appearing in front of the audience for the first time?

The throat becomes parched from nerves, the stomach is churning, and we hold onto a piece of paper as though it were a lifebelt. We feel like the link between our mind and our tongue has been lost. Time goes by infinitely slowly and fears and doubts are seething inside of you.

At that moment we are so bereft of something to hold on to that we try to find some sort of authority. We want to approach one of the famous clowns, sportsmen, or artists who are closer to us in terms of their world view, or to our boss, or an intelligent friend and so on. Many of us get caught at this level until the end of our lives, leaning on the names of famous and respected people under any given circumstances.

Unfortunately, this not only happens to clowns. Theatre artistes will make reference to Stanislavski, to his famous 'I don't believe you!' or to one of their respected teachers. If you ask a theatre artiste delicately why they are playing a role a certain way they will, most likely, answer you with a phrase that has also become well-known: 'That's the way we were taught.'

Moreover, not just actors will tell you this, but cinematographers, directors, and lawyers as well as representatives of many other professions. This response almost always seems pompous. It is used to garner some legitimacy, as well as coming from fear of taking responsibility. It seems to me that the aim of any teaching is to enable a student to grow their own wings.

The same thing happens with any presentation, with lectures, and with video conferencing.

Our minds are looking for templates. We lean on templates as if they were invisible props. By living and acting in accordance with templates, we are living or acting someone else's life on stage, someone else's role.

These props become shackles on our feet and prevent us from taking flight.

At the start of the journey this is not so bad. But how can we avoid being trapped at this level—how can we break out of our shackles and take to the air?

RULE 2

Don't put up boundaries!
The different possibilities are endless.

Let's recall again the first man on Earth. For Adam, the state of a clown was ideal. Judge for yourself, he doesn't know anything. He does not know that water is water, that earth is earth, that sky is sky. Furthermore, Adam doesn't know that he is Adam, that his hands are his hands; he doesn't know what is right and what is wrong. Adam is not chasing after his own success, or anyone else's.

Adam knows almost nothing, but having said that he does have a connection with the Divine.

At some point I read these words in the Old Testament:

'The Lord God made all the animals on the earth and the birds in the sky, and led [them] to man to see how he would name them, and so that man would christen every living soul with their own name.'[2]

The Divine is asking Adam himself to give all the animals and birds a name. And Adam did not have anyone to ask, he did not slip onto Google, or Yandex but invented all the names for the beasts and the birds himself. Furthermore, the Divine was observing him and did not intervene.

Is this not an artistic state of being? Is this not a state of having 'freedom of choice.'

There are several levels to this. If we think back to our clothes in the suitcases, it becomes clear what I am trying to say. Each of these items represents our qualities: our fears, our greed, our desire to dominate, our insatiable curiosity and so on. In each

[2] The Five Books of Moses, Chapter. 2.

of these qualities there is something animalistic. But nothing comes of the suitcases themselves, of vanity, since vanity is a purely human invention. When a personality trait manifests itself there is nothing negative within it, but when vanity is added to the mix this same quality becomes toxic.

Let's look at our qualities in their purest form, for now, without adding vanity into the mix, taking animals as an example. A dog is always hungry and spends the whole time sniffing everything, a hare is afraid, a donkey is stubborn, cats are their own selves, self-willed, a lion is proud and so on. These traits among the different animals demonstrate to us the diversity of the natural world.

Now let's look at these self-same traits in humans, when vanity is added in.

For example, people are afraid of appearing on stage because of their desire for success, as a hare would be. Or because of their insatiable curiosity they are always sniffing something out, like a dog. Or they are stubborn like the donkey, acting like a petty tyrant in their desire to appear to be a strong character. Or they are proud of their past achievements, which today are no longer relevant, and so on. We can find these analogues in almost every fable written by the most diverse fabulists.

In every context these traits turn into a poison, because we lose our precious energy not on artistic pursuits and creativity, but on something that satisfies our vanity. If anything goes wrong, we are caught like a fish on a hook of self-pity and depression. We can see these same parallels in other cultures as well.

My friend, Sandakva, is an Indian from the ancient Wendake tribe. The Wendake tribe live in Quebec.

Sandakva means bald eagle (a bird of prey from the hawk family that lives in North America). The name of his tribe though, the Wendakes, when translated into Russian means 'island of the giant turtle.' Sandakva and I worked at Cirque du Soleil for ten years in the show *Totem*.

Sandakva told me that according to his tribe's conventional religious beliefs there are two wolves fighting in every human being: a black wolf and a white wolf. Sometimes the white wolf wins, sometimes the black wolf.

My friend, Sandakva. Sandakva and I worked at Cirque du Soleil for ten years in the show Totem.

The white wolf symbolizes a person's pure spiritual state, while the black wolf is a symbol of destruction.

The white wolf in us represents our virtues, the black wolf our flaws.

Sandakva explained that animals represent human qualities. For example, the eagle is a Spirit messenger. They fly beyond the high mountains and connect man with the Spirit, with a great force of some kind that is within us and which connects us with our soul. The eagle sees things as though from a distance. After all, when we are consumed by a problem of some kind we do not see the problem as a whole, only a part of it. In order to examine the problem from different sides, we need to rise above it and perceive it as if from above, on a different scale. When this happens we see the solution to the problem. The eagle symbolizes this.

The bear is a researcher. When they get to a new location they do not eat anything, but check if there is enough berries and fish. Only after establishing that there is food in abundance does the bear settle in that location. When the fish and berries have run out the bear moves on to a new location.

The beaded lizard is a venomous lizard, one of the two most dangerous lizards in the world. It can live without food and water for a year, and what is more it spends much of its time underground. Hunters have smeared their arrows in this lizard's poison. The Indians attribute negative spiritual powers to the beaded lizard and this lizard can bring on diseases and problems.

Here the link to Adam is clear, at the request of God it was Adam who invented all the names for the animals. In our case he is naming the animalistic qualities in all of us. He gives each of these qualities a name. Why does God ask Adam to do this? It seems to me that it was so that Adam could remain Adam, so that he could remain in that unique virginal state, because only in that state would he have a connection with the Divine, with God. Without this connection he himself becomes just an animal leading a biological existence.

In order to avoid falling from grace he, with the help of the Divine, invents his own method, referring to each animal by name. As soon as one or another trait appears Adam already knows its name, is aware of its taste. He tells himself: that's vanity, that's greed, or naivete, or fear and so on. He puts everything back in its place whilst remaining in that wonderful state.

Only in that wonderful state do human limitations disperse and endless possibilities open up: we can act in a way in which we are oblivious to other people's opinions. We become independent of our, or anyone else's, tyrant-like behaviour, of their self-pity, stubbornness, self-will, pride and so on.

BEING ADAM

Rembrandt is my inexhaustible source of inspiration. All my static scenes and views I have glimpsed in the work of this great artist. His paintings, especially his self-portraits, almost immediately immerse you in the state of the Invisible Clown. For me being Adam means to experience this state.

What prevents us then from being Adam?

I went specifically to the Mauritshuis Museum in The Hague to look at Rembrandt's last self-portrait painted in 1669, the year of the artist's death.

I arrived in the piercing state of the Invisible Clown. This experience, however, unfortunately disappeared rapidly after just a few seconds and I decided to move on to another hall. After some time I understood that I wanted to return to that self-portrait. I again stood before this work of art and experienced the state of the Invisible Clown. After a short while this state left me once again. I began to analyze why I could no longer remain in it. Then suddenly I realized that my mind was constantly throwing up different ideas about Rembrandt, about this painting and about the people that were looking at it or were walking past it. My mind was saying: 'Look at the right eye, it's a lot brighter than the left eye. What was Rembrandt trying to say here? Maybe that his substance was hidden deep in shadow, as the left eye is a symbol of substance, why is it in shadow?'

Or: 'Look at the movement of the paint around his right eye, it's clockwise…. Maybe the artist wanted to say that his personality is symbolized by his right eye?'

Or: 'Look at the triangle between his eyebrows, maybe Rembrandt is drawing our attention to his third eye?' And so on and so on. Imagination and a constant interplay of thoughts were separating me from the Invisible Clown like a veil.

Our thoughts are our bodyguards on the way to the wonderful state of the Invisible Clown.

Some thoughts were sufficiently noble, but even they did not bring me into this state, and then I decided that I would just look at the painting, casting away any other thoughts, even the most scientific, the most noble, and the most poetic.

The longer I stood in front of the painting the more actively I was troubled by other thoughts: 'Well, why are you standing in front of this painting? What will people think of you?' Or: 'Give your place to someone else, they also need to look at this painting.'

I did not give up though. A short time later, and completely unexpectedly, as if by an ocean wave, I was engulfed in a feeling that I cannot describe here. No words have been invented to describe it.

Invisible Clowns live behind our train of thought. Any thought, even the most joyous, pleasant thought, separates us from this state.

This is very easy to understand with sex. Thoughts during sex prevent us from sensing an orgasm on a deep level. It is pleasant for us, but as soon as we succeed in switching off our conscious mind the feeling becomes much more intense, and it is almost impossible to describe these sensations in words.

Having cast away any thoughts like Adam it is time to start again, and gradually, should it be necessary, to impose your own pattern. It is this that helps me when creating something new: in my case an act or a show, and in yours — maybe a new aircraft or spacecraft... This is the reason why I only have a few clown acts — I am slow to create them.

Nevertheless, thoughts are needed to create an act or a show; however, as a rule, the very first thoughts — those on the surface — are very often templates.

RULE 3

Don't trust the first thought that comes into your head, but wait for the next thought.

Nobody knows where our thoughts come from and where they go.

Usually, the second and even the third thoughts are deeper, more perceptive, and more accurate, and for a clown — funnier. Either that or you suddenly learn that another clown is using your idea (ideas do float around), but what of it? This idea is not yours and you have to try to put it out of your mind despite the fact that your mind will say: 'You invented this a long time ago, it's a classic already.' Or: 'Everything old is new again.'

Remember the rule 'Don't put up boundaries!' — the true variant of who we are will definitely make itself known.

LESSON 1 — ADAM

The aim of all our lessons and exercises is to get rid of at least some of the templates and bring us closer to our natural state. We have grown to love the shops selling biologically pure fruit, now I am suggesting you grow to love your natural state, cleansed of templates, of the clichés of perception. For this I have prepared for you my first exercise, 'Adam.' You will need a video camera or a smartphone, a notebook, and a pencil.

EXERCISE 1 ●

Imagine you are Adam, the first human being on Earth. In this state you don't know anything. You have yet to master language and you use sounds the way a hungry baby would.

You need to think up your own language based on your sounds. Look around your room. Find a name for yourself using your own sounds and the objects you have around you, and write them down, so as not to forget these names. Think up a short story about yourself and tell this story using your new language. When you are ready, record this story into the camera. The story itself is not important in this exercise, what is important is the state you are in when you are being Adam. Do not copy children, or actors who have played children. Have you recorded your story?

Let's now make the exercise a little more complicated. Add four different states: surprise, fright, sadness, and joy. You should end up with four short stories, all of which are different, and which you have told in your own language of Adam: one in which you are experiencing surprise, a second in which you are afraid, and a third in which you are sad. In the fourth story you are joyful.

Watch your video recording, and, even if you do not like it, your task is to accept yourself for who you are. Fall in love with yourself. I would also advise trying this exercise in the shower without a video camera or smartphone, when you are alone, and, like Adam, you are naked.

In the third chapter we will examine another trait — the desire for success.

CHAPTER 3

Success

From the second chapter we learned that the Invisible Clown lives beyond the limits of our thinking, and in order to reach them we need to empty out our 'vanity suitcase,' which is full of different kinds of junk — our non-existence, our manipulation, our desire to dominate, our fears, greed, and self-will.

In this chapter let's examine a little more deeply that quality, which is similar to fear, but, to be more specific, is the dread of being an unsuccessful person. We will also discover that success is an ephemeral and fickle thing, and learn what we need to draw on when success happens.

SUCCESS IS ILLUSORY

When I was studying to be a clown in Moscow we were trained for success, and we were even spooked: 'You might graduate from here as stars! Or you might be nothing at all!'

Our entire philosophy of life is orientated around success.

Almost every advertisement plays on your personal happiness. We are often intimidated by television ads. If we don't buy this lamp, then the way we are living our lives is wrong. If we do not watch this film, then we will be taken for fools. If we do not buy this t-shirt, we will not be in fashion, and so on.

People are afraid of being losers and as a result they become losers — living someone else's life, one that is imposed on them.

Everyone aims for success all of the time, they are competing for who is the coolest, the funniest. I even know of one case where one man died at an international circus festival in Monte Carlo after being awarded the silver clowning medal instead of the gold one.

His heart could not handle it: he was certain that he would win gold. His act was without doubt up to a gold standard, and it was unique. After the results of the competition were announced, he returned to the hotel and died of a broken heart. What happens in our lives very often does not happen the way we perceive it.

What is success though? How long does it last?

I know a lot of troubled businessmen, who back in their youth, instead of using their talent, which would really have transformed them and refined them as people, chased illusory success. As a result those people lost their faith in their own talent and they did not earn any money either.

Success is a fickle thing. Today it's there, tomorrow it's not. Even one and the same show can be received differently in different cities and countries.

It does not matter what country you are in: you can be successful in one and the same city one day, but the next day the public may not laugh or react as they did the day before.

Your act has suddenly been put on immediately after the trapeze artists, even though before it was in the programme as following the jugglers, and the reaction of the crowd is not so good. Where then is the success?

A technician happens to miss his cue or a baby starts to cry in the audience at an inopportune moment — where is the success?

A younger and more energetic performer appears and all the success transfers to them, and even though you are still standing on stage nobody is talking about you any more, their attention is all on the young performer.

Or you move on with a touring group from Spain where the public react so well that their laughter, whistles, and applause they drown out a huge orchestra.

Or you travel on to Holland, where the reaction of the audience is so quiet that you can hear your own breath. Naturally, you think you can't win over the audience and that the public do not love you. Even though the Dutch like you as well as the Spanish, it's just that the Dutch are a little more reserved.

You cannot depend on success: everyone fails sooner or later and may experience depression because of it.

What actually can you depend on?

I would suggest changing the goal and, instead of chasing success, *gift* your performance to the public.

RULE 4

Gift your performance to the public.

THE BEGGAR

Artists are always unhappy with the public. They complain: 'In England and Germany the public were very good. But here, not so much…' Or: 'Yesterday the public were amazing, but today…'

We are unable to comprehend that our art lives in the present moment, when we are on stage, and that there is no yesterday for our art. Despite the fact that I perform my show more than 300 times a year, for me it is all one and the same show. My clown does not even suspect that there was such a thing as yesterday. For him life is in the now, in these eight minutes over which the clowning act is performed.

In chasing success we run away from the here and now.

I know one aerial ring artist. She would go on stage dressed as a phoenix. She needed to be successful at each performance, as if it was the air she breathed. Behind the scenes she would berate the public, grumble, and say that the audience do not accept her at all. She would obstinately demand recognition from the public. You just try not giving her praise. She is a phoenix, one look and she turns you to ashes.

We worked together in one of the most beautiful theatres in Hamburg, Germany. The technicians had fixed one of the cables attached to her ring incorrectly ahead of the show. If she was just doing acrobatic exercises, the load on the attachments would have been sufficient and all would have been well. Success, the applause of the public, and their wild reaction were, however, not enough for the phoenix. She started to demand more applause. In her jerky movements she drew closer to the audience and hung over them. She was using her whole body to demand more and more applause.

That show was a charity show for an old people's home. The elderly grandfathers and grandmothers, their hands already tired from their long lives, tried to help the phoenix feel like a successful artiste as much as they could. One elderly grandmother even cried out: 'Oooohh...'

For the phoenix though this was nothing at all. As a result of her jerky movements and the colossal load, even the red sequins on her costume began to come undone in some places, and would slowly spin, falling onto the white heads of the elderly people, snowy from their old age.

At some point the cable gave way and the phoenix, along with her heavy ring, crashed onto the stage, and she lost consciousness. We had to bring down the curtain, halting the show. Thank God everything was fine. The phoenix paid for this behaviour, as she knocked her two front teeth out.

Her fall shocked the public so much that the show became very quiet and mournful. It was hard to carry on. The public's thoughts were on the artiste who had experienced the unfortunate accident. Every other act after the phoenix was just a sideshow.

The clown looked completely out of place and seemed like a humiliation to the elderly audience. In order that the public trust me, as they had in my previous shows, during the reprise, in which I performed immediately after the phoenix's fall, I had to change my sequence and even change the repertoire of my performances. My clown act became more lyrical. This gained trust and empathy and put me at one with the audience.

Another example. Once I complained about the public to one famous juggler, Darwin. I told him that the public that day were subdued, and were not laughing as much. Darwin answered: 'Well, what difference does it make? We earn the same wage. If the public were good today we would still not get paid any more.'

Darwin approached his performances pragmatically. He did not seek any favour from the audience, and according to him, he never experienced any fear before them.

He was only afraid of one thing: that his employer would not pay him for his performances.

Darwin valued every moment. He would write carefully into his contract how many minutes he was supposed to be on stage. This got to the point that Darwin would take his iPhone on stage and would switch on the stopwatch. As soon as the alert went off telling him that ten minutes had gone by, he would leave the stage. If there was a delay in the performance through no fault of his own, he would also leave. It was hard for the director to work with him, but the public really loved him. Darwin the juggler in this case represents the limit of thrift.

Although a healthy pragmatism does us no harm, I would like to return to the topic of service, since I prefer a different approach. My friend, Mr. Irreproachable, a famous circus acrobat once told me:

In Russian 'Adam' sounds like the verb 'TO GIVE.'[3]

In order to experience the state of the Invisible Clown you have to give. Adam wants to give and he does not want to TAKE. Can you imagine if it was the other way round, if the first human being on Earth had been called Take?

[3] Translator's note: In Russian, words are pronounced according to where they are stressed (emphasized) on a particular syllable. In the case of *Adam* in Russian, the stress falls on the second syllable, so the name is pronounced as 'AdAM,' rather than the English ADam. The verb 'to give' (otdat) is also pronounced otDAT, and so there is a correlation between the sounds of the two words, as well as the sense.

The arrow is pointing at the performer, at the 'beggar.'

It is possible that if this was the case, we would not be here and neither would Darwin or the phoenix. In our case all we have to do is to give, to gift our performance to the public — five minutes or an hour and a half it doesn't matter. When we crave success, we want to take the audience's applause, their laughter and their love from them. This actually is not very fair since we receive our wages, so why would we need to beg?

When we give, we share what we have now, and this is completely sufficient. Our motivation is so pure and positive that we no longer care whether the public will accept our gift or not, and whether they are going to applaud or laugh.

When we go to a birthday party and offer the host a gift that has been carefully wrapped and decorated with bows and ribbons, we give that gift out of sincerity, and we hope they like it.

The most important thing is our intention, our motivation.

SERVE

It seems to me that here we are approaching the universal topic of service: an attitude that helps us to change the world for the better. The arrow has changed direction. Now it is pointing towards the public. Up to this point the arrow was pointing at the performer, at the 'beggar.'

The arrow has changed direction. Now it is pointing towards the public. Up to this point the arrow was pointing at the performer, at the 'beggar.'

This relates to stage performances, but the same thing applies in everyday life.

Twenty years ago a lighting technician looked in on the dressing room of the Moscow Clown Theatre under the leadership of Tereza Durova, and a conversation ensued about the future. The technician said: 'First I will graduate from my university, then I will find a good job and, when I start earning

I will marry and then build a house, I will have lots of children, then I will change the world for the better.'

Well, I thought, that technician is so young — and he already wants to change the world for the better. I was in my 30s and I had not even thought about such things.

How though do we begin to change the world for the better? I am, after all, not a politician... The world, at first and even second glance, is completely unfair. For example: I opened Facebook one day and suddenly I saw my show on stage at one of the theatres in Hanover, Germany, but it was not me who was staging and performing this show, but my friend — let's call him Mr. Weakness — with whom I had shared the concept of this show two years previously. Back then we agreed verbally that Mr. Weakness would not use the concept of this show, but nevertheless he did use it, inviting another clown, also a friend of mine, as well as a director who is very respected in the clowning world, and the man behind many clowns in the former Soviet Union, Papa Lagerfeld.

Knowing me and my concept for this show, Papa asked Weakness: 'And would Misha not be against this?'

To which Weakness gave the traditional response: 'This concept is a classic already. This was being done before Misha. We will leave out his gags and acts.'

My well-meaning advice: do not trust anyone, even your friends, and agree to everything *in writing*. This will help you and release your friend from any temptation, and, maybe, and this is the most valuable thing, it will enable you to keep your friendship.

Incidentally, this is another well-meaning piece of advice: do not waste time on friendships with anyone who is deceiving you, or does not value you, or drags down your self-worth. You will not get the time back and you won't become friends anyway. There are a great number of people living on this Earth, and you will definitely find some true friends.

A conflict of interest and friendship are linked to the topic of service. When you serve, you are able to see what your friend needs and you try to help them. When you are a 'beggar,' you will not be able to see another person's needs, only yourself and your interests. The balance between 'yourself' and 'someone else' is what friendship is.

Here is another example: An excellent director, let's call him Mr. Irreproachable, once approached me to share his idea for a show with me. I saw elements of my own acts in his idea, and even the finale of the show was a copy of my repertoire.

Irreproachable wanted to see my reaction. 'Listen!' I told him, 'why do you want to be compared to me? Try to find your own act. There are endless variations out there. I will help you.'

I happened to have a card that Mr. Irreproachable had given me the evening before with his photograph on it. I turned it over, and on the back I wrote that he was not to use the concept for this show without my permission.

Irreproachable put his signature on the card and then had to rethink his entire approach. He finally found a unique finale for his show. The show turned out to be so successful that it won international awards. No one could accuse the director of plagiarism, as they would have been able to if he had moved forward with his original plan to copy my acts. The most important thing was that we remained friends.

When I approached my Invisible Clown to complain about Mr. Weakness I suddenly saw that the Invisible Clown is not predisposed to judgment, it lives according to different laws. It's like a sun that just shines for everyone, both good and bad. The sun just shines, just serves.

RULE 5

Serve.

This helped me see both Mr. Weakness and my own weaknesses, such as anger, judgment, and my sense of injustice in a different light, despite the fact that it is hard now to call our relationship a friendship.

These same laws also work on stage. We should sense what it is our public needs. For example, when you are performing, especially when the lighting is up in the auditorium, you see people who are standing, even though there are empty seats. You could request that people sit in these empty seats. A lecturer, on seeing an elderly man without any water to take his pill, can offer them a glass of water.

Simple social interactions like these draw a performer closer to the public.

When you think about your appearance while performing it's all about 'you,' and in this situation you are full of a variety of fears.

When you see what it is the public needs, that's when you are 'serving,' when you are 'changing the world for the better.'

Then a conscious person, or anyone who is striving to be conscious, is able to 'serve' and 'to give' like Adam. Otherwise the arrow only works in one direction, towards the 'beggar.'

In order to *give*, first you must *have*.

Everyone around us is serving one another, either consciously or subconsciously. Take a cup for example, it's serving us, we drink tea from it. Someone made this cup and that means they served us. Everything we see around us, either object or phenomenon, is all created to be of benefit to each of us, and everything serves each of us, even if we do not understand this. The self same thing is true of our public performances. In order to eradicate stage fright you have to replace the desire to please your audience with a striving to serve them.

The outstanding Persian Sufi-poet Jalal ad-Din Rumi once wrote:

"How long are you going to seek
a buyer for your words?"[4]

For me this wonderful quote means: how long am I going to perform so that people praise me, and when am I going to perform for the public, oblivious to their praise and their opinions, which are just a product of my imagination?

In another verse Rumi wrote:

"Once I wanted buyers for my words,
Now I want someone to take me for my words."[5]

This unbelievable quote suggests to me that we have to become our words. We have to become our actions. We have to become a performer, and not a beggar for success.

VISITING AN INVISIBLE CLOWN

Even though our Invisible Clown is always here, it is not easy for us to go and visit him in our situation. We can put on our best clothes, take some expensive gifts with us, but we might not get to meet him at all. We, in essence, are uninvited guests.

Some people attempt to achieve this using narcotics, a single tablet or a piece of a special chocolate or a mushroom is all they need. By these means people do actually encounter the Invisible

[4, 5] Rumi D. Treasures of Recollection. – M.: Realityweb, 2010.

Clown, but without working specifically on themselves. Deprived of their external stimulation they are not in any condition to meet this wonder of will.

The travel expenses, which we incur by using narcotics to visit the Invisible Clown, are very large.

We pay in terms of the rebalancing of our body, the loss of our positive emotions, and the destruction of our organism. Our willpower and internal focus disappear.

When we pay for our trips to see the Invisible Clown by making our own modest labour every day, our body, emotions, and willpower flourish. When we retain our youth for a long period of time, we can visit the Invisible Clown whenever we like. We are not invited to visit the Invisible Clown, but when we do show up, we are not turned away. When we settle in that space, we do not FEEL at home, we ARE HOME. This is because the Invisible Clown is our home, and he is whatever we are.

This world at first glance is highly unfair, but it is our chance, method or pathway, which gives us an opportunity to be a guest of the Invisible Clown. Like all methods, however, it has to be studied.

Therefore, the world is unfair, but how can we change it for the better so that it becomes our method, or our 'narcotic' that helps us realize who we are?

As we are limited and we do not see a bigger picture — we live in our own world.

'I don't know anything' or 'it's no concern of mine…' These sayings do a good job of communicating the essence of our universal egoism. Even though it's 'of no concern to me' we nevertheless see ourselves as the center of the universe and we feel like we are the hub at the center and the world revolves around us. Egoism itself is a part of pride, and pride is a part of vanity.

Only by changing ourselves can we change the world for the better, and sometimes this happens simultaneously.

Try to be conscious for a few seconds. You will see that in that space of time your internal world will change for the better.

Each time you are on stage, at an audition, or in the most day-to-day moments of your life, if you could be conscious for one minute you could yourself and change the world for the better. This is real service.

If your performance lasts five minutes, then try to change the world for the better for just five minutes, and it will change around you for sure.

How though can this consciousness be achieved?

What is consciousness?

RULE 6

**Experience the world as it is, on its own terms,
and in the present moment.**

Unbelievable experiences lie behind this rule. If you could
be conscious of these words for one minute, then you could
try the world's tastiest dish. You could listen to the best music,
which has yet to be written by any composer. You could see
beauty that nobody has yet described.

In order to achieve this you need to try to not let any
thoughts come to you at all, positive or negative, when you are
experiencing this. When I am on stage, I cannot let any of my
partner's discussions, or those of the audience, or the technicians
or anyone disturb me, and I cannot let any excitement on the
part of my partner, the audience, technicians, auditorium and
so on disturb me either.

Do not allow any comparison between yesterday's audience
with today's audience. All this will lead your consciousness
away from the present moment and will destroy the character
of your personality and timing, as well as your own presence
and your readiness to give and to serve.

*'Be sequential and always hold onto the present moment.
Any mood, or more to the point, any moment, is infinitely special
since it is a messenger from eternity.'*[6]

In this phrase, recalled by Johann Peter Eckermann as
coined by Johann Wolfgang von Goethe, there is a method and a
problem. We can solve the problem by setting ourselves the goal
of holding onto the present moment. We experience any mood

[6] Eckermann I.P. Conversations with Goethe – M.: RIPOL classic, 2020.

that comes our way, but we do not become hostage to it. We value every moment because it is a 'messenger from eternity.' This is clearly a connection with the Divine, with eternity.

When we *beg* we become hostage to the desire for success.

When we *serve* we are no longer hostage to success, we are MESSENGERS FROM ETERNITY.

LESSON 2 — THE GIFT

Therefore, happiness is hidden under a dense layer of templates, which have been persecuting us since childhood. In childhood, if you do something not quite the same way others do, you will definitely be the butt of jokes. Sometimes this is unpleasant, and so you try and act the way everyone else does to avoid being laughed at. Furthermore, templates come to you as a result of your upbringing and education. In one sense it is better to 'invent your own bicycle,' and open yourself up to experiences, and create your own clothes, than it is to live someone else's life according to templates. We want to be happy and successful.

These two wonderful desires of ours are actually templates themselves, the entire basis of which lies in the meaning of the verb to 'obtain/acquire.' In the end what we want is to be happy. In Russian, however, the word for 'happiness' sounds the same as the word for 'now.' That is to say happiness is always in the here and now. The fact that happiness cannot be personal is also interesting. It is no accident that when we feel happy, we have a strong desire to share this happiness with those around us.

Therefore, we can conclude that although we experience happiness on a personal level, this feeling does not like being alone, in one body; it wants to be poured out to everyone. When we are unhappy we, with the exception of some villains, are reluctant to share this state, we don't want to make the people around us unhappy.

Sharing our happiness is natural. We each have a degree of happiness every day, on a scale of one to ten. If happiness is only in single figures, then you need to share it in single figures. There is no sense pretending you have a score of ten, as that would be unnatural.

When we are on stage, or during negotiations, we want to get something, either applause or a contract. Based on my experience I would say that when we share happiness with the public or with our business partner we get more applause, and more contracts. Gift your performance to the public, gift your presentation to the company, gift your suggestion to your partner, and gift your audition or exam to the commission.

Gifting is a state of mind; it does not mean that you should give something to someone for free. It means that you are not striving to hear the applause, or the praise, or the criticism given in your honour. You just want to share your performance, gift it to the public, and that's all.

EXERCISE 2 ●▨▨▨▨▨▨▨▨▨▨▨▨▨▨▨▨▨▨▨

This exercise is called 'The Gift.' You will need a video camera or a smartphone, a gift box, a ribbon, and a writing desk. Your task is to dictate into the camera a short text: a poem, or the lyrics of a song, or an extract taken from prose, or a fragment of your future performance. A musical accompaniment is mandatory. Prepare an audio recording, let's say, of the song "Happy Birthday to You."

Put your text, written out on a piece of paper, into the box, and tie it up using the ribbon to resemble a gift.

Turn the camera on yourself, stand in front of it at a distance of two or three meters. Place the writing desk opposite you. This will be your stage. Switch on the camera, take the box, and go to your starting position.

Turn on the "Happy Birthday to You," it should play for only the length of time that you first appear, no longer than 40 seconds.

Face the camera and hold out the box that has been gift wrapped at arms length, like you would a birthday cake

Approach the desk, put the box on the desk, untie the bows and take out your text. When the music stops, begin to read.

The most important thing is your attitude. Your performance and your text should become a gift to your public. This creative process is your happiness, so share your happiness with your public! Do not fake it, be natural.

Try to do this exercise four times. Twice with the music and the gift box. Then twice more without the music and the gift box, simply and naturally: hold the text in one hand and read it as if you were gifting it to someone on their birthday. Try to make all your movements consciously, and separate them one from another.

Watch the video recording several times. In your mind try to separate yourself from the personality you see in the video. This is no longer you, it is the personality you imagined and which no longer belongs to you. In that state you will be able to assess your performance more objectively.

The templates through which we perceive the world are growths and interferences, which prevent our consciousness from manifesting itself. In the fourth chapter we will try to separate ourselves from our name, having sent our names into the auditorium.

CHAPTER 4

Divide and Rule

In the third chapter we discussed the meaning of success and we also examined our fears that are based on a dread of being unsuccessful. We changed our motivation, and instead of striving for success, we now simply serve. We gift our performance to the public, not waiting for their applause. We gift our opinions in meetings, without worrying what our colleagues might think of us. We gift our ideas in the office with the boss, with no uncertainties or ingratiation.

In this chapter I am suggesting that we split our 'ego' into three parts.

In order to find our Invisible Clown we need to understand how this Invisible Clown is different from a visible clown.

The words 'divide and rule' are attributed to Philip of Macedon. We can try to apply this great saying to ourselves to manage our weaknesses, fears and doubts, and our reduced or inflated self-worth. These words work on many levels.

For instance, let's take Mikhail Usov, that is to say, me. In fact we could adopt any name — the name of anyone reading this book. In order for you to acquire practical experience, I would suggest using your own name instead of mine.

Therefore, you use your name and I will use mine:

My name is Mikhail Usov, the name of a person who was born on this planet around 50 years ago. Is this person a clown?

Mikhail Usov has a specific build and voice, and his existence has rhythm. He has his limitations and his strengths.

Who is Mikhail Usov?

Let's try to define this.

Since I was given my name by my parents and was not born with it, I will tell you everything that I was *taught*: to walk, speak, write, draw, read, play, play musical instruments, hold a fork in the left hand and a knife in the right hand, study history, vote in elections, pay my taxes and so on — all this knowledge we will attribute to Mikhail Usov.

Who is a clown?

What I was born with: the colour of my hair, my body type and its dimensions, the sound of my voice, my character, the speed at which I perceive the world, my disposition (whether I am an optimist or a pessimist), my temperament and so on.

We will attribute these qualities to a clown.

Mikhail Usov — is everything I have learned
The clown — is everything I was born with
Mikhail Usov — is a critic
The clown — is a costume

This is anyone who plays their role in accordance with the qualities they were born with.

TO BECOME A OBSERVER

RULE 7

Be a member of the audience.

Before my performances I ask Mikhail Usov to go into the auditorium and just look, and not disturb or control the Clown.

I have definitely come to a realization that I don't want to be an artist any more than I want to be a member of the audience. That is to say I want to observe my Clown along with the real audience members, to observe and not perform. In this paradigm the Clown moves to a new level, he becomes deeper, more refined, and more unpredictable. Mikhail Usov the audience member moves to a new level as well. He becomes responsible for maintaining the *state* of the Clown, and this new objective transforms the Clown into an *Invisible Clown*.

Let's do this, however, in order. We will remain for now on Mikhail Usov and his Clown's level, and we will return to the Invisible Clown a little later on.

Therefore, on stage is the Clown, and in the auditorium is Mikhail Usov, the audience member.

In this configuration Mikahil Usov enables the Clown to live its own life, and, along with the audience, the Clown can be amazed by and laugh at itself.

This division between Usov and the Clown enables the Clown to manifest himself. The Clown after all has no idea that Mikhail Usov exists. It is interesting how Mikhail Usov and the Clown are linked to one another isn't it? If Mikhail Usov forgets about himself for just three seconds the Clown would no longer exist.

The key word here is 'FORGET.'

In general memory, or our recollections, are key to our internal work on our personality, and also on our own selves.

After all, anything can happen.

SHOW #111

On the 111th show *Totem* at Cirque du Soleil I fell into the auditorium: I did not notice the edge of the stage because of the brightly coloured studio lighting board, and I fell off the edge of the stage along with my fishing boat. The enormous and heavy fishing boat covered me along with all the stage props, which were waiting their turn, carefully arranged in the boat.

Inside the boat were: aluminum saucepans of different sizes, fishing tackle, an anchor, an electric grille, a bottle of fake wine, a packet of milk, a green plastic onion, and a huge prop of a fly named Mimi.

The full-size single seat wooden fishing boat, which is on wheels with the base of the boat sawed off for my feet to pass through, covered me completely. The noise from the boat falling and the rattle of the saucepans, which was amplified by a microphone in the buttonhole of my shirt, gave rise to raucous laughter from the audience — 2,750 people.

'What an amazing special effect! You only get that with Cirque du Soleil,' said my friend, the Crystal Director from Leipzig who had been at the show. He should have known by then that I had fallen into the auditorium by accident.

The technicians rushed up to me, placed the boat back on the stage, placed all my props back inside it, and helped me to my feet. I sat in the boat and thought to myself: 'My arms, feet, and head are in one piece. Mikhail Usov go into the auditorium....'

Interestingly the Clown did not have any comprehension of what had happened. He, just like a child, had fallen over and started to whine in pain.

On the other hand Mikhail Usov had experienced a range of emotions: What would they think of me? I had fallen off the stage of the most famous circus in the world.

I will get fired. I can say now that I had a light bulb moment, no, I will say that the technician set the boat's trajectory incorrectly, no, I would frame the technician for it, and he would get fired. I would just say 'sorry,' and that would be the end of it.

This was all going on, before I remembered my Mikhail Usov, and sent him, his doubts, fears, and vanity into the auditorium. As soon as my dear Mikhail Usov was gone into the auditorium, the Clown sat in the boat and commenced his performance again as though nothing had happened. It all worked out: the nightmare visions of the future, which my mind was throwing up at me, had disappeared and the act continued successfully. The public did not notice my internal conflict, they were happy. I was anticipating that I would either be fired, or at the very least I would be reprimanded, but our artistic director said: 'That was really funny, you're a great clown.'

At times like these the memory plays a key role. My friend, the acrobat Unconditional, who is known around the world, wrote above his dressing table in large letters:

REMEMBER

Remember who you are, and also, if necessary, remember who you are not.

Remember what prevents you from being a good clown — and where these fears come from.

Remember the need to send your Mikhail Usov into the auditorium.

Remember this very moment, which is happening right now around you and within you.

REMEMBER THIS MOMENT

It's a paradox you might say? How can you remember a moment that is happening right now? At what point have we forgotten about this moment?

This happens to us all the time. We live in our ups and downs. We are not able to be conscious of ourselves all the time, just for a few seconds. A thought then comes to us a few seconds later, which takes us away from the present moment. We really do need to remember who we are, so we can attain that sense of being, of 'I AM.'

Try it right now. How long can you maintain your focus?

If we were to leave Mikhail Usov on the stage with his Clown he would certainly be afraid, begin to doubt himself, or start to criticize, comparing that show with one that happened before, and comparing today's audience reaction with yesterday's success. He would try to repeat the previous day. If he didn't hear sufficient applause and laughter, he would definitely criticize the public. There is no place at all on this tandem for the Clown, and in his place Mikhail Usov would be playing the role instead.

MIKHAIL USOV'S CALLING

If Mikhail Usov goes into the auditorium the question arises: is there an area in which he could actually help us?

Undoubtedly he would help when he is not controlling, but assessing the situation. For example, the public are inert, but he suggests increasing the rhythm, increasing the length of the pauses and so on. Also, as soon as he sees that Mikhail Usov is back on stage, he would advise him to return back to the auditorium. That is to say, he is protecting himself from himself. He is advising remembering this moment.

The gargoyles and chimeras of Catholic churches remind me of this. Gargoyles are located outside a church and chimeras are located inside. They defend the church from its enemies.

In us, there are external and internal enemies, and it is still not known which of these is the stronger. Our thoughts are examples of these internal enemies, and it is a complete mystery where our thoughts come from and where they go.

HOW OUR MIND INTERFERES WITH OUR WORK

I am a clown and a juggler. I juggle a ping-pong ball with the help of aluminum saucepans, hung around my body. The saucepans, are hung everywhere: on my shoulders, like a general's stripes, on my feet, in my hands and even on my head, like Don Quixote. This is how my mind interferes with the performance of my Clown.

When I am juggling, standing in front of the public,

sometimes the thought comes: 'You're going to slip up now.' If I pay attention to this thought I certainly do slip up. As soon as it appears, I say to myself:

'Mikhail Usov, Get back to the auditorium!
I am the boss here!'

Either that, or you go on stage and a thought tells you:

'You are portraying your character in a
completely unconvincing way.'

Then you would certainly feel like you are no longer convincing, or, as they say at the circus, you are unrestricted. Instead of simply doing what your role demands, you are beginning to analyze your character.

As a rule this character is then destroyed in front of the public's eyes. The Clown disappears and all that remains on the stage is your imagination, dressed in a clown costume.

This division between Mikhail Usov and the Clown is wonderfully applicable to any situation. Let's say I am a baker and my name is Frank Volkenbrot. The aim of the Baker and Frank Volkenbrot are completely different. The Baker wants to bake tasty bread. Frank wants to sell this bread and earn money, but he has lots of competitors. Everyone knows that it is not easy to bake bread, and it requires attention to detail, precise timing, and a level head. Suddenly, out of nowhere, Frank Volkenbrot appears with his thoughts about his competitors. At that moment the Baker disappears and our 'businessman' continues to bake in a completely mechanical way. Naturally, he will miss lots of significant moments in his work. As a result his bread will not be as tasty as it would have been had the Baker prepared it.

Frank Volkenbrot is also very important, but at the right time, and not when he is baking bread. There is a time for everything. At some other time Frank may give some thought to who he would like to sell his bread to, and how.

Our situation is so absurd that when Frank Volkenbrot begins, at the right time, to think how he is going to sell his bread and to whom, the Baker suddenly appears and advises Frank to add more olive oil to the dough.

Or let's say I am a doctor by the name of Doctor Demidrol, and instead of the doctor offering treatment, Doctor Demidrol interferes, he sees an opportunity to earn something from the patient. He intimidates the 'patient', prescribing a treatment for liver disease with tests every six months and so on and so on.

From a comparatively healthy person Doctor Demidrol has transformed his patient into a desperately sick one. Furthermore, the doctor disappears and Doctor Demidrol takes his place entirely.

If they have their wits about them, his 'patient' would decide to approach the other doctor and, if he is lucky, he will meet a sensible physician who will just advise him not to eat sweet fruit at night.

When this 'patient' asks Doctor Demidrol: 'How can this be? Where did you get that diagnosis?' Doctor Demidrol will answer in the time-honoured way: 'That's the way we were taught.'

Michel de Montaigne, the author and philosopher of the French Renaissance era, in his book 'Experiences,' describes similar situations with doctors, many of whom, back in the 16th century, he called charlatans.

Or to bring things up to date: I am writing this text and Mikhail Usov has one aim, while the writer, the author of this chapter, has a completely different one. A writer wants to get their message across, to share their knowledge, while Mikhail Usov wants to become famous with the help of this text, to remain in people's memories and so on.

Some time later Mikhail Usov may become tired of writing, he wants coffee and to scroll through Facebook and so on. The author meanwhile, like water, does not resist, he has no mechanisms for resistance and Mikhail Usov is taking up the entire space.

We should continue to educate our Mikhail Usov, as if he were our child, and instill in him the correct set of rules. This process is never ending, and we should love it. In order to love this process, however, we need to come to love our Mikhail Usov, in some sense of the word, as 'our very own.' We need to love him as if he were our own child. Talk to him. Rodney Collin writes about this in his wonderful book *Mirror of Light*.

*'In order to love, first of all you should love yourself.
In order to love yourself you need to accept yourself
with all your weaknesses, as well as your strengths.'*[7]

In our case we can say to our dear Mikhail Usov: 'Do not disturb the writer for exactly one hour, and then you will have 15 minutes to drink coffee and scroll through Facebook.'

Based on my own experience I can tell you precisely: Mikhail Usov also gets distracted, just like a child would. I gave myself an instruction to write for exactly one hour, but after exactly two hours I suddenly found that I was still writing.

WHAT'S ME, AND WHAT'S NOT ME

When I was studying to be a clown, we were often told:

'Don't play, be a clown or live the role.'

When you send your Mikhail Usov into the auditorium and he becomes a spectator, the Clown actually remains on stage but he is not acting at all: he does not even have a clue of what role to play, and he doesn't know that he is standing in front of the public, he just exists.

Thus, the Clown is on stage, while Mikhail Usov is in the auditorium. How then do we find the Invisible Clown?

He really is, after all, invisible. He is not of the world, not of this world in any case.

The Clown and Mikhail Usov will never be able to meet.

Here you could say that the previous chapters discussed visiting the Invisible Clown, and looking for the Invisible Clown within yourself, and now it turns out that Mikhail Usov doesn't

---

[7] Collin, R. Mirror of Light. – M.: Chernyshev Publishers, 1997.

have a chance. For the reader's sake Mikhail Usov is as much a product of our imagination as he is a real person.

I should explain myself at this point. As a human being each of us is divided into a number of parts: we are divided into our emotions, our intellect, our motor functions, our substance, our personality and so on, and Mikhail Usov and the Clown are merely parts of one whole. These parts cannot meet the Invisible Clown.

This is like Moses who had been leading his people in the desert for 40 years. When they reached the Promised Land God would not allow Moses to enter. He could not even set foot on this land. Moses was to die at the age of 120 on the 'threshold.'

In our case the Promised Land is the Invisible Clown.

The figures leading us there, the Clown and Mikhail Usov, cannot set foot there.

Either that or it's the other way around: the Clown and Mikhail Usov are functions, and the Invisible Clown is our consciousness.

The distance between our functions and our consciousness is not so great as the distance between a real flower and a plastic one.

It's a paradox, but in order to meet our Invisible Clown we have to become Invisible Clowns ourselves.

It is very difficult to explain this phenomenon in words, but I will try and find the words we need in poetry.

The verse on the next page by Walt Whitman from "Song of Myself," helps us to understand the substance of an Invisible Clown on a deeper level.

'My dinner, dress, associates, looks, compliments, dues,
The real or fancied indifference of some man or woman I love,
The sickness of one of my folks or of myself, or ill-doing or loss
or lack of money, or depressions or exaltations,
Battles, the horrors of fratricidal war, the fever of doubtful news,
the fitful events;

These come to me days and nights and go from me again,
But they are not the Me myself.

Apart from the pulling and hauling stands what I am,
Stands amused, complacent, compassionating, idle, unitary,
Looks down, is erect, or bends an arm on an impalpable
certain rest,
Looking with side-curved head curious what will come next,
Both in and out of the game and watching and wondering at it.'[8]

Whitman says directly that all this bustle that surrounds our lives, is not Me.

Here is another wonderful saying from my third teacher, the King of Hearts:

'I am the one who observes, not that which observes.'

This is who our Invisible Clown is.

[8] Original Text: Walt Whitman, *Leaves of Grass*
(Philadelphia: David McKay, 1891-92): 29-79. PS 3201 1891 Robarts Library.

THE CHARACTERISTICS OF AN INVISIBLE CLOWN

He has neither shape, nor colour, nor sound, he does not even have a smell. It is difficult to write about him, since even with two eyes you cannot see him, and with two ears you cannot hear him. If I were to say that it is possible to sense the Invisible Clown, then this would also be false. Have you ever seen the Grand Canyon? When you park your car and approach the precipice of the canyon and look down... The Invisible Clown is activated by what you see, but only for a few seconds; these few seconds of experience are a greeting from eternity, because after that Mikhail Usov is activated, with his 'ooh' and 'ahh,' which eclipses this indescribable experience.

That which Mikhail Usov is feeling is an experience of time; an experience of the state of the Invisible Clown, which happens to us very rarely — it is an experience of eternity.

Or you meet a girl and something is drawing you towards her, while Mikhail Usov actually finds no interest in her.

Or your long-awaited first child is born, and you cannot fully comprehend what has happened. Even on that day when the child is born and even at that moment when you were entrusted with cutting the umbilical chord, and you, like a clown in a circus, proudly, effortlessly cut through the umbilical with scissors, you still don't understand what has happened. The next day you sit in the car and travel back to your house, and on the way you suddenly realize that your child has been born. You are in such floods of tears that you cannot control the car any longer. Although once again Mikhail Usov interrupts you quietly and affectionately, suggesting the idea that you have to stop and buy sweets for the midwife. The tears dissipate, together with the wonder of the Invisible Clown, and Mikhail Usov returns to the stage.

Or you are in the Louvre: there are so many tourists standing in front of the famous Mona Lisa that it seems like the entire Louvre has come into that hall the same time as you do. It is very difficult to approach the painting, but soon enough you get a chance. You stand in front of the Mona Lisa and in the first few seconds the Invisible Clown comes on stage and you begin to see something that is beyond words. Mikhail Usov, however, does not sleep, and there he is. He does not sustain that higher plane of experience and, like the other tourists, decides to take a selfie. Unhappy at the flood of tourists Mikhail Usov forgets about the Invisible Clown.

Satisfied with just a selfie against the backdrop of Leonardo de Vinci's work of art, Mikhail Usov feels tired and he decides to get some refreshments in the buffet and does not feel up to the Mona Lisa, or the Invisible Clown.

You may well ask: 'What is the Clown doing all this time?' As soon as Mikhail Usov appears on stage the Clown disappears. When the Clown disappears the Invisible Clown vanishes immediately. As you have probably already noticed, there is a direct connection between the Clown and the Invisible Clown.

The Invisible Clown does not have fears, or doubts, and he does not tire, nor does he have a reduced or inflated self-worth — all these are attributes of Mikhail Usov. Even if you do not experience the state of the Invisible Clown, your knowledge and small amount of experience of this feeling will help you, in times of fear and doubt, to send your Mikhail Usov into the auditorium.

Evidently, experiencing the state of the Invisible Clown at will is very difficult. This is possible, however, as the Invisible Clown responds to beauty. The beautiful moments in your life, when you are observing nature, or enjoying sincere conversations with friends and having a cozy time and drinking some tasty wine in a lovely glass taken from some wonderful glassware, visiting museums, exhibitions, or decorating your home will bring you closer to this encounter.

A phrase coined by Fyodor Dostoevsky, 'Beauty will save the world' acquires, in this context, a new meaning.

Mikhail Usov cannot endure competition with beauty, but, unfortunately, after a few seconds, thoughts will appear, which may or may not be noble, or on the other hand may deprive you of this unbelievable experience. As for me, I have understood by now that it is best not to say a word. It is better to be silent, drive thoughts away and to drink in this joy — an encounter with the Divine.

LESSON 3 — SEPARATE YOURSELF FROM YOURSELF

When we stand in front of the video camera, either as a viewer or when we are in the course of negotiations, it is worth separating ourselves from our own name, at least mentally. You will become unbelievably interesting and nobody will be able to take their eyes off of you. This very simple thing, my favourite exercise, will help you to 'separate yourself from yourself.'

EXERCISE 3 ●

You will need a video camera, so that you can record the whole process, a chair, post-it notes, and a pencil.

You will need to read a small text into the camera, which you read previously in the last exercise. Some verse, or an extract taken from a song, or a work of prose, or something from your future performance.

Turn your face to the camera set at a distance of approximately two to three meters from you. To the left of you identify a location, maybe one or two meters from yourself, and place a chair there. Now the most important thing: is to imagine that this chair is not a chair, but your own name. Let's say Ivan Ivanovich Ivanov. To make it more obvious, stick a post-it note with your name on it onto the back of the chair.

Have you stuck it there? Excellent! Now concentrate. You are going to dictate your extract. Before, during, or even after you have dictated your extract to us, thoughts will definitely come to you. To begin with it is not necessary to write down every single thought, but any time any thought comes to you, stick a post-it on the back of the chair. It could be any thought, like 'What is this load of rubbish that I'm doing now?' or 'What is the viewer going to think of me?' Or you may hear a sound or see an object, which brings an association to mind, and then a thought.

When you have finished your dictation, just keep standing in silence doing nothing. You need to stand for three minutes, focusing on the emptiness, and not on your thoughts. That emptiness is YOU. Do not be afraid of that emptiness, and on the contrary, start to love it.

Every time a thought or an association appears, stick a new post-it note onto the back of the chair. A thought may even come to you as you approach the chair or the video camera, and if it does, just continue to stick post-it notes onto the chair. When you have finished the exercise, look at the number of stickers. More often than not these are your templates, to which you react somehow or other and which close you off from yourself. Do the exercise again, and now imagine yourself in your mind adding thoughts to the back of the chair. They are just thoughts, which belong to your name — they are not you. You stand to one side and observe both your thoughts and the process of your dictation. You — are not your name. You — are the one who observes. You do not assess, but observe. Your name is the one who is doing the assessing, your Ivan Ivanovich Ivanov. And the individual who is doing the observing, is YOU.

Do this exercise for no less than three minutes. Your dictation should take no more than 40 seconds. When you assimilate the essence of this exercise you can do it again, recording your thoughts on the post-it notes. I promise you: it will be very funny and illuminating to see your thoughts.

Try to practice like that on a walk, or on public transport, separating yourself from yourself, mentally sticking your post-its onto an imaginary chair. Watch your video recording. Similarly, separate yourself from the personality who stood before you in the video. Whatever you do not like about this video is your name — it is not you. Try to watch the video without criticizing it, detached from it in such a way as though it were someone else performing. In this state you will be able to assess your performance more objectively.

CHAPTER 5

The King of Fate

From the fourth chapter we learned how to separate ourselves from ourselves, and how to send anything that relates to our name into the auditorium, and how to become a member of the audience, observing the performance of our Clown. We also learned how these important actions lead us to the state of the Invisible Clown.

Since all four chapters of this book have been more about teaching, I would like us to take a break for a little while in the fifth chapter. I will tell you about the first time I went on stage, as well as about my first teacher, the King of Fate.

THE FIRST TIME I WENT ON STAGE

My first performance took place in the drama hall of Kharkov's school No. 78. I went out on stage with a German Weltmeister accordion on my chest. I was eight years old. As I was very afraid of meeting the gaze of my schoolmates, I planned to go on stage with my back to the audience.

At this school concert, which was dedicated to the 1st May celebrations, the worker's holiday, I played the waltz 'Waves of the Danube.' I wanted to turn to face the public right in front of the stage on the first notes of the chorus, and I was thinking that when the time came it would not be so scary. This grandiose plan, however, was not to come to fruition.

As soon as I appeared in front of the public, I felt an invisible pressure pressing down on me. At the rehearsal I had counted the steps, there were precisely eight of them. As a result of the horror that had gripped me, however, I lost count and I did not notice that I had reached the edge of the stage with my back to the audience, and I fell over the edge in a crash.

Falling off the stage, as you have noticed, is my 'party piece.' My classmates were falling about laughing. I decided not to give up and, overcoming my fears nevertheless, I began to play the chorus, lying on my back: 'Tratata-tratata-tratata-ta…'

My father then said to me: 'We can't all be musicians.'

The phenomenon of fear has interested me since childhood. My classmate Semyon Ogurtsov bought a cupcake in the school buffet for 15 copecks. We were both seven years old. All I could see was the top part of this delicacy and it was pinky-white, like foam on a Christmas tree decoration, a cream meringue.

It was as though I began to hear an internal voice that had appeared in my head: 'Would it be wrong to take the top off his cake?'

'And would it,' I thought, 'be bad?'

After plucking up the courage I drew level with Syoma, and with my seven-year-old fingers I quickly tore off the meringue in such a way that the only thing the young boy had left in his hand was the cup cake made from a short pastry. I had swallowed the cream. Semyon was powerless in his surprise. After mock fighting for a short time we became close friends.

Later on in my performances I used this same approach, which is based on surprise. We, as clowns, often do animations. These animations are a direct interaction with the public. When we are on stage, the audience is all but invisible to us because of the bright lights, but animations are completely different — this is eye-to-eye and it is the element of surprise that defines success.

For example, at the circus we do PR acts with the press wherever possible: at the town hall, on the town squares, and on the streets. On one occasion we performed one of these events for the press at the office of the Mayor of Moscow, and even the former mayor Yuriy Luzhkov joined in. I, as a clown, was asked to mingle with the guests. In my hand was a large bamboo stick, a clown's baton, which was designed so that whenever anyone is hit with it, either a viewer or a stage partner, the stick makes a loud noise but it does not hurt anyone. At some point the Mayor drew level with me, and my Clown, without thinking, hit Yuriy Mikhalich around the head with this clown's baton. The knock was loud and the guests fell silent. The bodyguards immediately took my baton from me and began to poke around it, checking it. Luzhkov, however, was not angry, he ordered the bodyguards to give me back my baton and for them to leave me alone. I had noticed a long time before this: if a clown alone is involved in such provocation, whatever you do is never offensive. It is worth Mikhail Usov getting involved though, as this could be interpreted as a personal insult.

Another example of a PR-act using animation takes place at a railway station. All around us are people with their suitcases. You offer to assist someone by carrying their case up to the platform, and they trust you with their baggage, and you quietly begin to run away from them, carrying their suitcase. They begin to run after you and the entire station turns into a theatre stage where everyone is involved in what is happening.

THE TRAIN DRIVER

In view of the fact that I didn't attain such good results in school, I was not accepted into the 9th grade. In my family it became a real issue over what I was to do with my life.

I dreamed of traveling and I had a strange idea of becoming a train driver. I submitted my documents to the railway technical college. Everyone at home was against the idea, every one of them tried to tell me scary stories about trains and accidents on railway transport. Could they convince me otherwise, however? Stubbornness is a personal characteristic of mine.

My mum hatched a clever plan. She bought us two tickets on the train from Kharkov − Vladivostok − Kharkov. This journey took 18 days. To begin with it was so romantic and wonderful, the landscapes changed, the conductors in the carriages changed shift several times, and the people around us changed, along with their stories.

One guy carried two fighting cocks in two large bags. With their crowing at five o'clock in the morning, they woke every passenger in the train. The guy would take some water in his mouth and spray it over the cockerels. They did not crow when they were wet. As soon as they dried out, however, they would scream loudly again. It was because of these cockerels that nobody in our carriage had got any sleep since dawn, and the queue for tea and for the toilet had been a long one from six o'clock.

Another passenger, who was traveling from Kazan to Novosibirsk, told us an interesting story about how he had met his wife. He was a musician, a pianist and, in his own words, the best performer of Beethoven's 'Moonlight Sonata' in the Kamchatka Regional Philharmonic Orchestra.

The pianist had married for the second time. He had married the wife of a famous pilot and cosmonaut, twice Hero of the Soviet Union Saturn Marsianovich Moon. It happened like this: the cosmonaut was invited one day to a concert as an honoured guest of the philharmonic. Our musician played the 'Moonlight Sonata' at that concert. Sitting alongside Saturn Marsianovich at the concert though was the pianist's then wife, Strawberry Cupidonovna. By chance they happened to strike up a romance. On realizing this the musician decided to settle things with Saturn Marsianovich.

He knew the car that they were ferried around in. The pianist sat in wait for an ambush near the hotel in which his rival was staying.

When the car pulled up, the musician jumped out from the garden, but instead of Saturn Marsianovich the cosmonaut's wife Venus Mercuryevna Moon, an indescribable beauty got out of the car flirtatiously.

'And this girl was just like the Moon, when it turns to a full Moon on the fourteenth of the month, she had a light blue dress on and a green scarf on her sparkling brow, she stupefied the imagination and bewildered anyone of sound mind...'[9]

Nobody could resist when presented with such beauty. Our musician could not resist either. He invited Venus Merkuryevna to the 'Space' café situated across the road from the hotel, which, in the pianist's opinion, served the best ice cream in the Soviet Union.

The wife of the cosmonaut almost immediately noticed the pianist's hands. His hands were wonderful, but not just wonderful. The musician had famous hands. These famous

[9] *One Thousand and One Nights.* – M.: Khudozhestvennaya literatura, 1975.

hands, however, were not famous for playing the grand piano. The musician told Venus Merkuryevna how his hands had been specially filmed for a famous film about Lenin. In this film Lenin's hands were shown in close-up when he wrote something or picked up a glass of tea. The famous actor, who played the role of Lenin brilliantly, did not have very nice hands. So as to show the leader of the revolution in the best light possible, the hands were filmed separately.

For this film our musician, or more accurately his hands, even received a state prize.

The pleasant acquaintance of such diverse people as Venus Merkuryevna and the pianist grew into deeper relationships.

As a result of this story Saturn Marsianovich and the pianist swapped wives. Strawberry Cupidonovna became the cosmonaut's wife, while Venus Merkuryevna became the pianist's wife.

Our journey with my mother continued, and to begin with I was very glad that I had submitted my documents to the railway technical college. 'You see, Mum, you see,' I would announce to my mum almost every day. I even said that the railway is something famous. It is such a shame that we are not allowed on board the locomotive.

On the fifth day I had grown tired of being thrown around. The main thing though was that you had just met people, you had only just started to make contact with them, and then they were gone for good from your life. My stomach began to ache. I could not wash… On the eighth day I wanted to go home. Even the buffet car did not save us. We wore ourselves out on that long journey. When I got back to Kharkov, I picked up my documents myself.

Mum advised me to go and train as a construction metal worker. Mum thought that metal workers were well paid.

In order to really convince me, Mum took me to work at her workshop for two months as a metal worker's assistant.

I do not remember much in that workshop because I was almost immediately fired. I remember that one metal worker in the lunch break sliced his salami directly on the workbench, and I was salivating. In the Soviet Union at that time salami was in short supply, and the metal worker did not share his with anyone.

As I was a man of humour another metal worker, Tereza, that's how everyone knew her, sat me on the cutting lathe, the runner, put it into low gear and took me for a ride on it, like a father takes his children for a ride on ponies in the park. The foreman of the machine shop saw all this. I was fired for violating the technical safety rules.

What I really enjoyed though was that everyone was laughing at me. In view of this joyful atmosphere I decided to become a metal worker, and we submitted my documents to professional technical college No. 14. It was boring though at that professional technical college, and nobody was laughing at me any more, they would only very occasionally laugh at me in an underhanded way. This was a different sort of laughter, and not a kind one.

THE MEETING

The metal worker's trade turned out not to be my dream, and what that was, my dream I mean, I still did not know. I understood very clearly though that I did not want to live like my parents did. Going to work that they did not love.... Most likely I would have stayed working at that factory, but maybe I would have died long ago from anguish and alcoholism. The Divine, however, was clearly intervening in my fate. The King of Fate entered my 14-year-old life as if from nowhere.

I met the King of Fate at a bus stop. He was tall, bald, with a soft gait, and the Cheshire cat's smile from *Alice in Wonderland*, carrying a leather briefcase, which contained almost his entire life's drawings of a new stage prop, and children's attendance registers, which he would be constantly filling in and filling.

In an enormous thermos he had his black tea with thyme, honey, and lemon. The steam and its wonderful aroma mixed with the smells of caramel from sweets, oat biscuits, and crackers. The King would share all these goodies with us children at the end of each lesson. His attentive and modest wife would make the tea, the Queen of Fate.

In the pioneer's and school children's center, the King of Fate led the circus society. This society was a ray of light in the Soviet city of Kharkov, not only for me but also for many, many children and young adults.

The King would say of himself, 'I am a crank.'

He was my first real teacher, in contrast to my form teacher in my first class in school, Amber Amberevna Pattern. This teacher's surname illustrates the fact that she looked at the world, and at us seven year olds, through a template. She had several favourites, but she viewed everyone else with surprise: why had they been born into this world?

If Amber Amberevna did not like, for example, our long hair, she would grab us by our hair and shout something for a long time. What it was she shouted I do not remember, but I do remember the disgusting, cold spray from her saliva. It seemed to me that Amber Amberevna Pattern was unlucky in love.

From this I concluded: wherever there is a template, there is no love.

ROOM NO. 24

The King of Fate approached me himself at the bus stop, and in place of a usual 'hello,' he uttered words that took me by surprise.

'Young man, tell me your mother's name and patronymic.'

'It's a scam.' I thought, but I said out loud:

'Baronessa Oberfeldt.'

'And where might I find Baronessa? Do you have a telephone at home? Tell me your number.'

I did naively give our telephone number. He called on Sunday. He asked to speak to my mum.

'Misha, some polite circus man called, he is inviting you to the circus, to circus training. He told you to bring your gym shoes and sports kit.'

Mum, well what am I, a clown?'

'That's up to you.'

Exactly one week later on the following Sunday another call came through:

'Baronessa Oberfeldt, please.'

'Misha, it's your circus man again. I will speak to him...'

'Mum, well what am I then, a clown?'

Every Sunday for a month, at around 10:30, the King of Fate would call our number, he did not give up, and softly, softly he convinced my mum. He was actually a juggler, and if a juggler does not succeed and the objects he is juggling fall, he would just patiently pick them up again and repeat his act, until he gets everything right. That's how he was with me, and he got his way.

I gave in. I took my gym shoes and sports kit and arrived at the pioneer's center where the King of Fate held his lessons. A grandmother in glasses stood at the door doing her knitting.

Without taking her eyes off of four needles, on which hung half a sock, she gave her command:

'Room No. 24, second floor, up the stairs on the right.'

I went up to the second floor. On an enormous white door was written the word:

SMILE

On the door hung a yellow sun that had been cut out of plywood, and the sun was smiling.

I opened the door. It was a huge light room with high ceilings. The guys of around my age or younger were throwing juggling pins or rings in the air, somersaulting, doing handstands, riding on rollers, or riding unicycles, juggling with knives, hanging on the trapeze, or doing the ladder act. Two beautiful girls wore light coloured silk dresses, and a boy on his own sat on a mat doing splits, while another was walking the tightrope with a Chinese umbrella. Another girl was flipping over backwards, while another was spinning 20 hula-hoops at the same time.

Standing against the wall, like a god, dressed in a sports kit and fashionable trainers, holding the plastic lid in his hand from his thermos, was the King of Fate, controlling this entire dynamic process, which at first glance resembled complete chaos.

He said softly:

'Natashenka, pull your sock up. Volodenka, straighten your shoulders. Seryozhenka, keep your hands parallel.'

Next to him was a reel-to-reel tape recorder, which he would switch on and off periodically. From the speakers the music of the composer Georgiy Sviridov rang out, 'It's Time, Forward!'

The King of Fate personally greeted me. He took me by the arm and led me to the dressing room. I changed into my sports kit and I felt uncomfortable in it, particularly in my gym shoes. This was the first time in my life I had put on shoes like these. They are like slippers you wear at home, but they are not slippers. The gym shoes stretched my entire sole and at first it was very uncomfortable.

The King of Fate looked at me and said, 'Your arms and feet are like twigs, we have to pump them up. Andryushenka, help Mishenka pump up his arms.'

What struck me was that I, possibly, had seen light for the first time. My childhood was spent in the Soviet Union. On the streets of Soviet cities a grey light dominated everything, particularly in autumn. Only occasionally would the streets lighten up on the national holidays, with banners and red flags. There were no advertisements either. Moreover, you would come across instructions such as these in the form of coloured placards:

TAKE CARE OF NATURE!

A MATCH IS NOT A TOY! or

GLORY TO THE KPSS![10]

Light and colour have the most powerful influence on us after all. When I first went on tour overseas to Germany and found myself on Reeperbanstrasse where the theatre we were working in, the Schmidt Tivoli, was located, my head started to spin and my legs gave way from the abundance of light and the colours on the advertising placards on the streets. I collapsed, losing consciousness for a few seconds. A crowd of sympathetic Germans gathered round me, who helped me get myself back on my feet and recover.

Here in Kharkov in 'Smile' I saw an abundance of light. All

[10] *Translator's note: the KPSS is the Russian for 'Communist Party of the Soviet Union.*

the circus props and costumes were colourful, with sequins and bijouterie.

I was 14 years old and for the first time I felt at home.

I don't know why the King of Fate chose me and why he had approached me at the bus stop. You cannot escape your fate. Most likely the King of Fate noticed my figure. I was short, thin, and a little ungainly. At the very first lesson the King of Fate tested me so as to draw out my talents. He asked me to perform a somersault forwards and then backwards, checking my flexibility, and then pronounced his verdict, 'You are going to be an acrobat — a bad acrobat. You are going to be a clown.'

Although the first lesson lasted no more than two hours, I always remember that day. When I left the King of Fate passed on his regards to my mum and my dad in a quiet voice, 'Mishenka, say a big hello to Baroness and Baron Oberfeld.'

He was like a clown himself. Old posters were hanging on the walls of room No. 24. On one of these posters the young King of Fate was sitting with everyone's favourite clown Yuriy Nikulin. One of the children had poked out the King of Fate's eyes with a ballpoint pen. When the King of Fate saw himself without eyes in this photo he flew into a rage. He organized a meeting of all the children and their parents. I thought that he was going to say it was vandalism. The most important thing that was bothering the King, however, was:

'Why did you poke out your teacher's eyes? Why not Nikulin?'

I could barely contain my laughter.

'Is Nikulin your teacher?'

'Natashenka, why did you poke my eyes out?'

'I did not poke the eyes out!'

'Mashenka, why did you poke my eyes out, why not Nikulin?'

'I did not poke your eyes out.'

He asked each of the children, but nobody owned up to it. After the meeting his wife, the quiet Queen of Fate, removed the poster so that it would never again remind the King of this humiliation.

Despite his eccentricities, he taught me and many other children to love what we do. The King of Fate would often tell us stories of one old circus attendant in the Kharkov circus, who painted the sawdust.

Previously, as now in the progressive circuses in the West, the circus ring would be covered in sawdust. This circus attendant painted two buckets of sawdust — one bucket in red, and the other in green — and before each show he would decorate the ring with sawdust and, with the help of this sawdust, he would form the shapes of two enormous red tulips.

After the first equine act, no trace of this sawdust remained and, therefore, there was no point to this decoration of the circus ring; and more to the point, nobody had asked this circus attendant to do this. Every day, however, over the course of many years he would gift his tulips made from sawdust to the public as a first impression of the circus.

It seems to me that unwittingly this circus attendant was a poet.

Public performances are very similar to painting the sawdust, while circus performances are even akin to painting the AIR.

If you are an artist of a film director then your work — either paintings or films — will be accessible for a very long time, and not just to one generation. We just perform in the here and now in front of the public. Our art just lives for a moment. We leave the stage and our art leaves with us, until we are back on stage again. For one thing this creates an appreciation of our performance and our profession.

SELF-WORTH

A real teacher, like a good parent, lifts their student's self-worth, helping them to grow their own wings. Occasionally, however, without intentionally bringing down their self-esteem, things do not work out for the teacher, because after all they have one goal: to teach. Let's say they may, frustratingly, not pay the student any attention for a long time. This helps them with humility. I have used this more than once on stage. You become smaller as a result of humility, and the smaller you become, the more the public loves you and the brighter your character shines.

When a teacher lowers a student's self-worth, however, with the aim of raising himself up to show the student what a great teacher he is, this is not a true teacher. Walk away from them.

In my life it was the King of Fate that gave me hope, showed me I had wings, which every one of us has who believes in themselves, and performed a 180-degree transformation of my fate.

The King of Fate passed away. I do not know whether he entered eternity. I did hear a story though of someone who, after death, entered eternity and thought it was a mistake as he had led a far from righteous life. He had not caused people any particular pain, but he felt that having entered eternity he did not belong there.

Then he plucked up the courage and approached St. Peter:

'It seems a mistake to me that I am in eternity.'

St. Peter looked at him, put on his glasses, took his enormous card-index, found that person's story and said:

'It's all correct, you have done exactly what we called you to do.'

'What was my calling?'

St. Peter looked again at the card index and said:

'Do you remember 15 years ago you went by train from Moscow to Warsaw?'

'I remember.'

'In the train you went to the buffet car.'

'Possibly.'

'Do you remember a woman with a baby who sat opposite you?'

'Possibly.'

'Do you remember that woman asked you to pass her a salt shaker and you handed it to her?'

'Possibly.'

'That was your calling.'

This story shows us how important every detail is in everything we do. Every little act of kindness that we do could be our CALLING. Letting another person go before us may be our calling. Or letting someone else let you go first could also be our calling.

The word 'calling' in itself sounds pompous and suggests something grandiose. Living the simplest life you can though, doing the simplest things you can, or just doing good, is what our calling is.

The King of Fate lived a complex life, but it seems to me, a happy one. He followed his calling and left behind him his wonderful students, many of whom even up to now perform with their own acts and shows across the world. Those students, whose fate was not to become circus artistes, became great people. The King of Fate taught us to love. For that may his memory live forever.

CHAPTER 6

The Secrets of a Clown

In the previous chapters we learned how we are able to conquer some fears, insecurities and our self-belief, as well as become happier, with the help of the Invisible Clown. This is a practical chapter. This is about how to enter into an audience with the Invisible Clown with the help of precise timing, and how timing is important for any undertaking.

TIMING
is the regulation of speed, rhythm and frequency
to achieve the desired effect.

It seems to me that clowns know better than other artistes what timing is; after all, they depend on it. Without the correct rhythm the public will not laugh. A clowning act lasts for approximately eight minutes, and if something has gone wrong the public will sense this immediately and will not follow the performer's lead. In view of the fact that a clowning act does not last very long, a clown is able to check the results of their work very quickly.

Anyone who goes on stage should study how clowns use timing. Prior to working at Cirque du Soleil I was a freelance entrepreneur, that is to say, I chose where I was to perform and when. I had to write 50 emails a day to potential hiring managers. I did not always receive a reply, but when I did receive one the employer would use it to ask about my terms and conditions and other important details. I had to respond to these messages in good time. If I answered immediately, my message, as a rule, would not be thought through, was very emotional and contained too much information. If I delayed the response, the employer would find other clowns instead of me and I would again lose the chance to find myself some work. Then I understood that my business, selling my clowning act, functioned according to the same laws as those that apply on stage. If an entrepreneur does not complete their business tasks in good time, their business will not grow.

Therefore, effective use of time ensures that the entire mechanism functions properly, independent of what it is we do: whether we are putting on shows, engaging in clowning acts, leading a theatre or a large corporation, conducting an orchestra, or just simply cutting the grass or chopping wood. Doing everything at the right time is the key to success. In our bodies, when the vital organ, the heart, is working perfectly, it supports the function of the entire organism.

It is common knowledge that making people laugh is much more complicated than playing a dramatic role. The road to making people laugh passes through perfect timing. If a joke is told at the right time, the public will find it funny. Timing is the principal secret for a clown.

In order to know this secret, however, you need a better understanding of a clown's profession. Just what is a clown?

It is not possible to answer that question succinctly. A clown on a theatrical stage, or a variety stage, is one thing, and in the circus ring quite another; on the street it is different again. What unites them all, however, is the need to observe accurate timing.

Visitors from another planet

I asked my clowning friends what being a professional clown means to them.

Atami Noda Batista

A student of the Gran-Canaria clown school, Spain:

'To see the world as a tragedy, transforming it into a comedy.'

Yevgeniy Voronin

The maestro Voronin,
a Ukrainian-American comedian and juggler

'*A professional clown is someone who is able to remember and repeat their successful improvisation. A pro knows how to pick up and invent jokes and tricks, and what is more, thread them into a coherent narrative.*'

Peter Schaub

A German-American comedian:

'The work of a clown is to make people laugh.'

Marc Antoine Picard

A Spanish clown,
and a clowning teacher at Cirque du Soleil

'A clown is someone who has found their true selves. A person who accepts themselves — their strong and weak sides — completely, and as a whole, and because they have accepted themselves, can share laughter with others; and if they don't make them laugh, they will at least touch their hearts.'

Jon Monastero

An American clown, script-writer,
and my partner in the show *Totem* at Cirque du Soleil

'*A clown is a fool, a phony, a wolf, a sheep, the sun and the moon, laughter and tears, a liar, and someone who tells the truth. A clown reminds us that there is no sense in taking life so seriously, but more than anything a clown — is an idiot, who bravely opens their human heart and soul, reflecting in them all the glory and the horror of life. They fall and suffer failure a million times, and yet they do not lose heart, and this reminds us that we need to try and get up a million and one times.*'

Aleksey Mironov

Clown and film actor, Germany, Russia:

'The disposition of a clown — is joy and composure.'

I asked **Houch-Ma-Houch**,

A Ukrainian-German clown,
what he thought of a clown's view of happiness:

'Happiness is going on stage, to see how people look at you attentively, react, feel sad and laugh along with you. When you work for a long time on a project of some kind, you think, when is this all going to end. Then a month goes by without a show, and you understand that you just cannot live without this. Without going out on stage you feel unhappy.'

This is what the Encyclopedia of clowning and performance art has to say about what a clown is:

'A clown – ... is a circus artist, a performance comedian, who performs satirical acts at slapstick comedy events, they are eccentrics, comic actors, and specialists in the grotesque and in parody. A founding trait of the work of a clown is the ability to invent comic images, situations, and tricks. To think like a clown is to possess a special gift of being able to substitute the logic of common sense with the logic of witty comparisons, associative links, and paradoxes. A personal comic style plays a defining role.'[11]

I agree with all of this. It seems to me that real clowns are a little out of this world. It is highly likely that they are aliens who arrived on our planet especially so that those of us living on Earth don't take ourselves too seriously. On Earth children become adults, while for clowns it's the other way round: from adults they become children. At present there are 256 countries on Earth. The Divine has sent each of them a clown-alien. The majority of clowns, however, ended up in Germany. More than likely because this is a very serious country and the other countries no longer have any need of clowns.

Often journalists who interview clowns are interested in one and the same question: 'How does a clown differ from an actor, and in general, is an actor a clown?'

In my view they are and they aren't. Usually an actor works with a large number of people. A dramatist writes a play for them, a composer writes the score, and a director gives the whole creative process direction. A good actor should realize the author's vision.

A clown is more often than not the dramatist, the director, and even occasionally the composer.

[11] http://www.ruscircus.ru/encyc?func=text&sellet=%CA&selword=807

An actor one day might play the role of a jester, but the next day they could be playing King Lear. A clown does not play anything, they just ARE. Inside, as with everyone, they already have their King Lear and their jester, and the comedy and the tragedy.

It seems to me that a good clown is a poet. A poet of action, an artist of living pictures.

THE THREE FACTORS BEHIND SUCCESS

At the heart of anything are three factors: **timing**, the **character being created**, and **state**.

TIMING, as we examined above, is a sense of time, or rhythm. Or that which can be defined by the interrogative 'When?'

CHARACTER is the essence, the structure, and the goal of whatever we are doing. If we are on stage then this is the essence of the persona, their habits, and reactions, their attitude to the world and to themselves. Character can be defined by using the interrogatives 'WHO?', or 'WHAT?,' as well as 'FOR WHOM?'

STATE is consciousness, or, a conscious perception of the world on its own terms in the present moment. It is our state of the Invisible Clown; the most suitable definition for him would be: 'HERE' and 'NOW.'

Recently I met a very successful businessman, a publisher from St. Petersburg. He had been attending my master classes for two years up until our meeting.

He told me that his business is doing very well because he has built his entire enterprise on the principle of 'timing — character — state.'

• In order to publish and sell books he needs to know the best time to do this, and which book should be published and sold at a given time;

• He has to know precisely when to secure business meetings with his partners, or his subordinates;

• He has to clearly define a strategy to publish a book, what its topic is going to be, as well as the design, the costs involved, and so on.

What is most interesting is that this approach is most effective when the publisher does this consciously. Thanks to consciousness he avoids making rushed decisions, he does not allow himself to make any false moves with respect to his partners, authors, or his subordinates.

It seems to me that accurate timing decides almost everything in any undertaking. Sometimes the window of opportunity opens up, and it seems like we are not prepared for it. If we do not take these opportunities that have opened up before us, new opportunities will not be quick in coming.

Let's examine how this works, using my profession as an example.

If I have created a very good character and I know for sure that I have good, funny jokes,

I must work on problems with timing. That is to say, I do not tell the joke at the right time: I either hold back, or I am a second too early and therefore the joke doesn't work. I know this is my weakness. It's more than likely I would not last a minute on stage. The public, like an X-ray machine, would read my character, and after that I would just become boring to them.

If everything was fine with my timing but, unfortunately, I had not succeeded in creating a convincing character, I would be in a much more fortunate position and I could act in a play, or, if I wasn't a clown, I could give an entire lecture. The public would forgive me because they would not get bored with me. It is possible that it would not be an outstanding work and would be forgotten the next day, but I would be able to see the play, lecture, or act through to the end. I would avoid failure.

I know quite a number of performers who have precise timing, but their characters are so bad that the audience is able to learn almost nothing of their persona. Nevertheless, these artistes enjoy specific success because of their timing. Many large show-business corporations are following this path. It takes a great deal of time and work to create a really good character. As we know, in any business time is money, therefore the directors rely on timing and often turn a blind eye to developing a character. These shows do quite well but they are not remembered, they do not stand out from the others. They do not become works of art and they are simply run of the mill.

When timing, and a character's persona work together to achieve a result, we feel much more comfortable. There would be much more harmony in what we do and we would find real joy in our work. We could appear in films, on television, as well as work on the most prestigious stages in the world and command the fees we deserve.

Another level of performance exists, and if we master it then we will not need to work on our timing and image any more. We will become a mystical actor, clown, or troubadour. That is all we have to do, just maintain this level and not worry, not about timing, or character; on the contrary, all our concerns would turn into a barrier and would interfere with us attaining this level.

WHAT THEN IS THIS WONDERFUL LEVEL?

This is the state of the Invisible Clown — CONSCIOUSNESS. This is our presence, our true selves. Although this is a very big goal, the ultimate goal of our learning, as my dear teacher the King of Hearts once said:

> *"Everything is just getting started from that level,*
> *and it never ends."*

Therefore, timing is a rhythm, a sense of time… the sense of a pause. It is the breath of your enterprise, your clown, your act, or your show. Timing is the basis of anything.

Sometimes I succeeded in discovering a very successful and funny character for my shows, but without accurate timing my jokes did not work.

If we are to compare timing to the layout of the human body, then timing is the skeleton.

I have noticed that people, who perform occasionally, especially clowns, mistake a sense of timing for speed — and they simply start to do everything more quickly, or they go to the other extreme and they perform more slowly. To do everything more slowly or more quickly is not timing. Accurate timing is when everything happens at the right time.

It is true that sometimes the public are sleepy, or sad, seized by a single emotion. This happens when the viewer is under the influence of the new or full Moon, cosmic phenomena (such as Mercury retrograde, meteorite showers and so on) or by our earthly problems, let's say, when a very famous person passes away. Or a very simple example: in Germany in March when people submit their tax declarations and learn how much they need to pay in taxes, the public are downcast. In order to cheer them up everything has to be done a little more quickly, but the sense of timing nevertheless needs to be solid.

You go from idea to idea that you plan to deliver, or from joke to joke, keeping the end goal in your mind.

If you do not know how to make an entrance on stage, go to your first idea that you want to share. There was a moment in my life when I had little clowning experience, and I needed to make an entrance on stage, but I did not understand where I needed to look — into the auditorium or at my partners or at the ceiling or the floor. My then director, the wonderful Tereza Gannibalovna Durova, who saw my confusion, told me: 'Go to your first gag.' That is to say, to your first joke. This means keeping your goal in mind of telling your first joke. In that situation it is not important where you look. You have a goal and this leads you on.

Here we are approaching an understanding of the 'ULTIMATE GOAL.' As the author of this term put it, one of the founders of the Moscow Arts Theatre Konstantin Sergeyevich Stanislavskiy, the ultimate goal represents the main idea, the goal, and the objective, from which the play, the actor's image, or the show is created.

Therefore we need to go from joke to joke, from topic to topic, remembering the bigger picture, or the end goal of the performance, of the entire enterprise. In my master classes I set a target and I give my students a dart. The students, in performing any sketch, keep the end goal in mind — hitting the apple with the dart at the end of the performance. In doing this they gain a better understanding of how the term 'ultimate goal' itself is maintained, as well as how to maintain their own ultimate goal throughout their performance.

You have to add energy to each of your movements. This is because any movement for anyone who performs in front of the public represents a whole event, and this movement cannot be just an empty gesture.

Disrupting timing for a performer leads to energetic failures; we call them energy wells. A weak clown tells a joke and the public laughs heartily — and hearing the public's laughter is very pleasing to a clown and they want to keep this moment going as long as possible. Therefore a clown waits while the audience laughs and tells his second joke only after this laughter has stopped. A good clown will not wait for the laughter in the auditorium to dissipate and would maintain the rhythm and tell the second joke at the right time, the most suitable time for that joke.

The same goes for other stage performers; a weak speaker takes their lead from their audience, for example, they wait for them to applaud. By doing this both the clown and the speaker lose rhythm.

A good performer works without keeping their eye on the public: they will take the next step to their idea or their goal when they need to.

Performing on stage is about mathematics. The number of jokes, ideas, and their succession are counted. For clowns, for example, the classic succession is the 'rule of three,' or as we know it in clowning language 'the law of two and a half.' We repeat one action three times, and on the third repetition comes the inversion, and this is where the joke is. There are exceptions to this. Any performance you give will come alive if you allow yourself to deliberately voice the stupidity out loud, to tell the joke for example. We do this when we need to take the pressure off the public, so we need to make a judgment call on this.

You cannot communicate two ideas simultaneously. Even clowns don't tell two jokes at once. First you communicate one idea and then the other. If you need to combine two ideas, you need a good reason for doing so.

Sometimes timing solves everything, and sometimes it is the character that has been created that solves everything. Our internal self, our Invisible Clown, helps us to recognize this.

Many performers are afraid of pauses and they are constantly working whilst breathing in.

They do this time and time again. But a pause is a part of movement. A pause is our breathing out. Often this is the motion of our soul.

Recently I attended mind-training sessions at Cirque du Soleil. I particularly liked one of the exercises. We were trained to breathe from the stomach, the way little children breathe. You have probably noticed how babies push out their stomachs; this is because they are breathing from the stomach.

In order to get rid of stress it was suggested that we breathe out six times, but only breathe in deeply, from the stomach, for four seconds. It seems to me that this wonderful plan demonstrates how important it is to breathe out.

My second teacher, the King of the Absurd, a clowning teacher (I will write about him in the second part) once said that clowns are paid for pauses, and I asked him: 'How can this be?' he answered: 'It's very simple....on stage, a pause puts your wages in the bank.'

Whatever you do, be it creating an act or working on a report, or preparing for an audition for some filming sessions, you have to consider two breaks, which will certainly appear in the preparation process. They will also appear in the performance process. Usually these are our weaknesses. You can read about breaks in Pyotr Demyanovich Ouspensky's book *In Search of the Miraculous*, where he discusses the wonderful system of the Fourth Way.

Thanks to this system any event or phenomenon happens in accordance with the law of octaves. For example, let's take the musical staff.

The musical staff is illustrated in the drawing below, from one note to the next. We can see black and white keys. You have probably noticed that between the notes MI and FA, as well as between SI and DO, there are no black keys. These are our two breaks. As I have already mentioned above, these represent our two weaknesses.

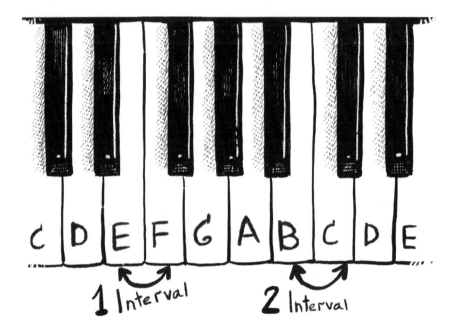

This illustration highlights DO RE MI FA SO LA TI DO RE MI and the first break and the second break and the inscription reads 1st interval and 2nd interval.

They are two weak places in anybody's consciousness and in our own performance. Knowledge of this in itself helps to destroy our fears.

Knowing about these problems, which inevitably appear almost every day during my performances, I have learned to transform my weaknesses into my greatest strengths. For example, the public shout something to you and you intentionally lengthen the pause. The situation is then transformed and miraculously turns in your favour.

Or, you are conducting a video-conference and at that moment the cat that you have locked in the next room meows, demanding you let them out. Everyone hears this. If you continue the video-chat pretending that nothing is happening, then the attention of the participants will shift to the cat. In the world of theatre actors, it is well known that it is impossible to outperform animals. If an animal happens to appear on stage, all the attention of the public will be concentrated on them.

So, if you are on a video-chat and the cat you have locked in the other room meows, the participants will not be able to make out a word you are saying and will just hear the meowing of the cat. You need to free the cat and accept it as your partner. Start to interact with it. The cat will cuddle up to you and you can stroke it, and in doing so you will gradually bring the attention back onto yourself.

Whatever we do represents the path of water. Water will always take on any form we want it to. This is what it means to accept the world on its own terms. We, like water, accept what the present moment is offering us, and we adopt whatever shape this moment puts before us. We are a higher power for water, when we, for example, pour it into a glass. We can drink water from a glass if we do not accidentally knock it over — in the same way the present moment also represents a higher power. We simply observe its terms, and if we do not do this, it will be like the story of the cat: an animal locked in a pantry, everyone can hear it, but we pretend that nothing is happening at all, that there is no cat there, and it is only our public that can hear it. In his story 'The Actor' Mikhail Zoshchenko's writes: 'The public are idiots.'[12]

Often this is how it is, but you would be an idiot if you did not notice the cat. My wonderful partner and friend the White Clown once appeared on stage with his act the 'The Mini Piano.' It begins with the clown coming on stage and standing before the little piano, greeting the public, waiting for their applause.

At one of the shows, however, after the White Clown had approached the instrument and turned to face the public, suddenly a huge buzzing fly, which was clearly visible and audible to the public, flew in. The White Clown also saw this fly. Without losing his head he made an entire event out of this moment, a whole clowning act. The fly flew here and there and the clown just followed it with his eyes: At some point the fly landed on the artiste's right cheek, crawled there for a few moments and flew across to the left cheek, and then again transferred to the right cheek and flew away. My friend did nothing and just followed this insect with his eyes. The public laughed themselves into hysterics. The White Clown just allowed the fly to be and was subordinate to this moment, having accepted its terms.

We will discuss this in more detail in the third part, 'State.'

To work on timing is to work on the subordination of your mind. The mind often rushes or is delayed because of an abundance of a sheer variety of thoughts. Apart from that, to give an order to complete or not to complete the next action our minds feed us an external idea of some kind, which does not bear any relation to the situation at hand. Therefore, be careful and do not let your mind interfere in the process, this is very

[12] Zoshchenko, M. Selected works. – M.: Azbuka, 2003.

important if you want to be a good performer. Not only if you want to be a good performer, however, but also a good person. I even wanted to put a full stop after the verb 'to be,' and this phrase suddenly looked like this:

'Be careful and do not let your mind interfere in the process, this is very important if you want to BE.'

Surprisingly this sentence has now found itself between two words that both mean 'to be.' Namely, 'TO BE' and 'I AM,' and what is key in this method: is that we DO NOT have any other way. Our consciousness disappears, immerses itself in our thoughts, and we find ourselves somewhere else, and not in the here and now.

'A human being is everything or nothing. It is not given to us to be in between.'

For me this thought means that when I am me, when I have a sense of myself, I am COMPLETE, and when I do not have a sense of myself, I am simply not there, correspondingly, I am INCOMPLETE.

LESSON 4 — DO EVERYTHING SEPARATELY

Let's start doing some exercises on the art of timing. Many people do lots of things simultaneously, and as such their characters are seen as restless and not very serious. More often than not this happens because our emotions go off the scale. When you perform in public, or, if you are simply participating in important negotiations, you will be taken much more seriously and your words will carry much more weight if you learned to do everything separately.

EXERCISE 4 ● ▬▬▬▬▬▬▬▬▬▬▬▬▬▬▬▬▬▬▬

You will need a smartphone, a metronome, a small writing desk, or any kind of desk, a file, in which your text will be printed in .pdf format from the first exercise, as well as a dart and a dartboard. Set the video camera or smartphone up opposite the table at a distance of two to three meters, and put the file containing the text and the dart on the desk. Hang the dartboard to the left or right of you. Switch on the metronome so that it works at a measured tempo, not too fast and not too slow.

All your subsequent actions need to be taken separately and at the right time, keeping in mind the end goal: THE TARGET. You should learn to do this exercise so naturally that your movements appear 'seamless.' For this you have to remember the goal, that you hit the dartboard with the dart. You have to concentrate on the target from the very start, from the first step.

Walk up to the table. Pause for a moment, counting the clicks of the metronome, 1, 2, 3, 4.

With both hands pick up the file from the table and hold it at the level of your stomach.

Pause for a moment: 1, 2, 3, 4.

During this and all other pauses don't forget to always keep in mind the goal — the target.

Open the file, again pause for a moment: 1, 2, 3, 4.

Read the entire text, then pause: 1, 2, 3, 4.

Close the file, then pause again: 1, 2, 3, 4.

Put the file on the table, then pause: 1, 2, 3, 4.

Take the dart from the table, aim, and launch it at the target,

then pause: 1, 2, 3, 4.

Move away from the table.

Do this exercise four times, twice with the metronome and twice without it. As soon as any thoughts appear don't forget to mentally stick a post-it note on the back of the chair, exactly as we did in the first exercise.

Whether you hit the bulls-eye or not is not important, what is much more important is to remember the goal. As with the first exercise, pay attention to the pauses between your actions. A pause is a part of movement. Our mind forces us to act in line with templates, to always work while we are breathing in, while a pause — is our breathing out. Charisma lives in spite of the mind — and it lives as we are breathing out, in the pause.

Watch your video recording. If you continue to do things at the same time, then perform this exercise again. You can do this until you are happy with the result.

Part Two

CHARACTER

CHAPTER 7

Who Am I Playing?

In the first part of the book, which is called 'Timing,' we separated ourselves into our name, the Clown and the Invisible Clown. We changed our motivation from a desire for success to a desire to serve, and we determined what the three main aspects are to anything, specifically to performing in public: timing, character, and state. We analyzed the meaning of 'timing' and we determined that it was the skeleton on which the whole structure of our activities hangs.

In the second part, entitled 'Character,' we will learn how character is linked to our charisma, structure, and style.

WHO AM I PLAYING?

I will try and communicate my ideas using a story about the profession of a clown. I don't just go on stage, I also lead my own small theatre and I am the director and founder of my own master classes. I have noticed that my method — timing, character, state

— works in every field in which I am active. Therefore, it can prove useful in solving completely diverse tasks.

OUR CHARACTER IS OUR MUSCLES

Recently I spent some time in the BMW museum in Munich.

The timing of this car is its speed, acceleration, and the braking distance.

The character of this car is its style, comfort, and safety.

The state of this car is its price, and the desire to possess this specific car.

If timing in anything, and in my case it is my work as a clown, is a person's skeleton, their character is their muscles.

Just as we need to maintain our physical strength and to constantly pump our muscles, we need to work on developing our character on a regular basis.

The best way to find your character is to observe people, animals, and nature in different situations. Our eyes and ears should always be open for 16 hours a day, even when we are asleep.

Once I watched a play called 'The White Guard' at the Mossovet Theatre in Moscow. I still remember almost down to the last detail an elderly couple in the audience. They were not sitting together, but either side of the aisle in the middle of the stalls, in the 11th row. The lady was in seat 14, while the man was in seat 15. Next to him, in seat 16, sat a beautiful young woman. He was clearly happy with his neighbour, and yet alongside his wife in seat 13, as if it had been kept that way on purpose, there was a vacant seat.

Before the play started they noisily agreed that if nobody were to come and sit in that vacant seat, he would move to sit next to his wife once the lights were beginning to dim in the theatre. When the lights had gone out, however, he had no intention of doing this. The lady in a loud whisper started to ask her husband to sit next to her: 'Albert, come here, nobody has sat in this seat, it's free.'

Albert pretended not to hear her.

'Albert, I told you come here, you wretch.'

'Bella, don't distract me.'

'Albert, sit here…You goat!'

'Bella, where is your sense of decorum?'

Despite the fact that the play had already started and the artiste was giving his monologue, Bella grabbed hold of Albert by the sleeve from across the aisle and began to pull her husband towards her with some force.

He did not give in.

'Bella, pack it in! You are getting in people's way and they can't see 'The White Guard.'

'You goat, we will sort this out at home….Just wait till we get home!'

'Bella, people are staring.'

'I don't give a damn about them. Why on earth did I buy these tickets? Look at Lenya from the third entrance to our block, look at how he treats his wife.'

As you have already gathered, an alternative drama had broken out in the stalls. An usher quietly approached the couple and asked them to be quiet.

Bella could barely keep her composure until the interval. No sooner had the lights come up than Bella set about shaking Albert out of his disloyalty and his dormant consciousness using her handbag and her fan.

These two people gifted me two characters, which even to this day I sometimes use in my performances.

Anyone who performs in front of the public should find their own performer in themselves.

Character is what your persona is made of, and also what surrounds it. Character is the habits your persona has, its reactions and its relationship with the world and with yourself. Character is the charisma of your persona. It is your performance style, your image, which consists of everything — from your hairstyle to your make-up, to your costume and your shoes, down to the last detail of your performance.

When you are preparing to look at the public, are you, let's say, wearing glasses? Are you looking through your glasses or over the top of them? How do you look at your watch and do you need to look at your watch at all? Do you need to raise your hand to greet the public, or is it sufficient to nod your head? Do you need to know beforehand what you are going to be doing, even if in the course of the performance you do the complete opposite?

Atmosphere plays no small role. How will the hall be set up that you will be performing in? What sort of lighting will be focused on you? Do you need to see the public's eyes and, with this in mind, is it worth switching off the lights in the hall? In doing so would you not lose the atmosphere, which is so important during performances?

After all, the right atmosphere is 50% of your success. Occasionally you do not have to do anything at all: the atmosphere itself makes your performance for you. This is used well at Cirque du Soleil. There any show is created on the principle of the four seasons: for the hour and a half of the show's duration the four seasons are always changing over each other. All of the circus acts, lighting, costumes, and even music are all dependent on the season to which the specific part of a show is dedicated. If it is winter then white and ultraviolet will predominate in the costumes and the lighting score. In this atmosphere both the jugglers and the acrobats will look different.

Cirque du Soleil creates the character, style and magic of its shows through the image of the four seasons. The public likely do not understand this, but they enjoy the beautiful atmosphere. This same atmosphere becomes a symbol and has an effect on the public's subconscious.

Music also has a bearing on character. What sort of music should it be? Classical or contemporary? Live or a recording? I love to use classical music in my performances. It does not distract the viewer from the concept of my clowning acts.

When the 'Russian National Ballet' brought its famous shows to California, I attended 'Swan Lake' in San Francisco. The ballet itself is unbelievably beautiful, and the performers are virtuosos. All the action, unfortunately, took place against a recorded score. Naturally you instantly feel this. Pyotr Ilyich Tchaikovskiy's outstanding music seemed dead because it had been played some time ago.

The public and the artistes are experiencing on a given day one and the same moment, one and the same season, one and the same cosmic phenomena, the same universal issues. It is these confluences that bind us with invisible threads and unite us as one: the dancers, the musicians, and the public.

If the music has been played some time ago, however, possibly back in the summer two years ago on a sunny day under different cosmic, or even political, influences, the wonderful music of Tchaikovskiy, let's say in autumn, would somehow sound different to the performance itself. A sensitive person would feel that and would not be able to enjoy it to the same degree they would if at the ballet the live orchestra, the dancers, the conductor, and the public could melt into one.

119

AS THOUGH

Once I carefully asked one clown to explain to me in words the character of his role. This clown distinguished himself by virtue of his wonderful timing and performed a number of circus tricks. Unfortunately, however, the character of his personality was poorly thought through. Surprisingly, this clown explained his character as follows: 'Well, it's as though I play a jolly person.'

He used the words 'WELL' and 'AS THOUGH.' This means that he does not know his clown, his character. We would hardly use the words 'as though' if we were acquainted with our personality on a detailed level.

It was true that this clown was always smiling during his performances. His eyes did not show any emotion and were empty, like those of a dried fish. He would draw his lips into a smile both when he did and did not need to.

Moreover, he would always be moving his lips, entertaining some dialogue that nether he, nor the public, could understand. He would often squeal.

Despite the fact that he would sprint on a wire juggling six balls, and the public would applaud him, it was 'as though' he was successful.

In our performance we should answer succinctly the question:

'Who is my personality?
Who am I playing?'

WORKING ON YOUR CHARACTER

The search for an idea

One of the ways of finding your character is to invent a biography for them, where does your personality come from, how old are they, what is it that they like, and don't like? Who are their parents? How do they view women and men? What is their favourite food, their favourite drink? You need to know everything right down to the make of the television in their home. Where they sleep and at what time, what their hobbies are and why they love them.

You need to ask yourself these questions and try to answer them. Interestingly, the answers to these questions can be found anywhere, in museums, on aircraft, in shops, and in books. You need to observe life and make it your habit.

Working on your character is easier in museums than anywhere else, because you can do this by looking at the paintings. If you already know the personality you need to play — let's say, a juggler, musician, or a doctor, you put into the search engine the search terms 'pictures showing jugglers/musicians/doctors,' and have a look through as many images as you like on this topic. You choose the most suitable variant for you.

We sat with the legendary costume designer Kim Barrett, who designed the costumes for the film 'The Matrix' for the (at that time) Wachowski brothers, and Baz Luhrmann's 'Romeo and Juliet' for two days on the Internet, trying to find the idea for an image of a fish for our Show Totem at Cirque du Soleil. For some reason, however, she saw a cabbage white butterfly. Thanks to this butterfly she came up with the vision for my costume.

Therefore, if you still do not know which character you want to play, you can still go to an art gallery. You will find your idea there. Let's say I know that red will predominate in my costume, then this will be the aim of my visit to the museum, and I will definitely find a small detail, which I can then use in my show.

SCALE AND RELATIVITY

One of the most important keys to creating a convincing character is to define their character's dream. In order to do this you need to understand the SCALE of a personality. For example, one person might be dreaming of buying a new sofa, another of becoming a cosmonaut, a third, the principal trainer of a hockey team, while a fourth of traveling to Tibet and becoming a monk.

The RELATIVITY of a personality is their weak or absurd side. For example, a desperado is always forgetting their umbrella. Or a superhero who saved the world from baddies has a shoelace that is always coming undone on their right boot.

'It's a single step from the great to the humorous.'

As Napoleon said, after he hit his head on the ceiling of his carriage during his retreat from Moscow along with his army. Let's make use of this phrase.

The larger the scale of the personality, the funnier their simplest problems can be. A personality is dreaming of the cosmos they will fly to in their space ship, but the rocket is full of everyday rubbish, which had been overlooked and not cleaned out when it was launched. In this example the bits and pieces float around our cosmonaut in weightlessness, and a superhero is fighting against them.

Or it may be the other way around, an everyday personality who dreams of just being left alone, and who just wants to sit on the sofa with popcorn and watch television shows. Suddenly, he is transported along with his sofa, popcorn, and television to the Tibetan mountains and ends up surrounded by meditating Buddhist monks.

FORM, TEXTURE, AND COLOUR

It is extraordinarily important to define form, the texture of your character, and even what colour they are. Picture yourself as a child of six years. What colour would you paint yourself in? What sort of personality do you have — a rounded or square personality? Is your personality soft or hard? What does your personality sound like, is it a bass, falsetto, or soprano? What musical instrument can you equate to this personality: a flute, a trumpet, clarinet, or double bass? Your costume, shoes, and, where necessary, your make up, will depend on form, texture, and colour.

ALOGISM

If you are performing as a clown, then alogism should be present in the character you have created. It is a very important component, because clowns see and understand the world differently.

The outstanding Russian clown of Armenian descent Leonid Yengibarov once said:

'If you never forget one thing it's when you're doing a handstand and you slowly lift one hand off the floor, and you understand that the globe is lying there in the palm of your hand.'[13]

This is very poetic and there is an alogism in it too.

---

[13] Yengibarov, L. The Final Round. – Yerevan: Sovetakan grokh, 1984.

Another great clown of the 20th Century, Grock, once said:

'I love it when I am being beaten over the head with a hammer, when it stops, you experience such pleasure.'[14]

Clowns break all laws legally. My clowning teacher used this example: you are taking your jacket off, you throw it up in the air and it sticks to the ceiling. For a clown everything is the other way around, even the laws of gravity. If a clown started to wash a saucepan with their hands, they would try so hard that they would rub a hole in the dishcloth.

Alogism, however, does no harm for any performer, not just a clown. It makes your character come alive and makes them interesting, because the public will not know how to read you. The public also live according to templates and logic, but when you disrupt the chain of events this remains in the public's memory and the ideas that you are sharing are better accepted and remembered.

Once at a large meeting with his students my third teacher, of whom I will write later, removed his boot and put it on his head. He said: 'There is every chance that from everything we have discussed here, you will only remember this moment.'

LESSON 5 — STYLE AND CLOTHING

Once I was entertaining the participants of an international conference of Nobel Prize Laureates as a clown. This conference was dedicated to new directions in culture, science and literature and was held in the Swiss city of Zermatt. Among the performers was John Lord, the British composer and keyboardist. He had been invited to perform because he had written the brilliant composition 'Smoke On The Water,' which had opened a new direction in music.

[14] Kukarkin, A. Charlie Chaplin. – M.: Isskustvo, 1988.

John arrived on stage in a dinner jacket (since this was a general requirement) but with black flip flops on his bare feet. It was this detail that lent him charisma and made his performance more memorable. There were an enormous number of famous people at the event, but I remember John Lord and that detail of his wardrobe more clearly and with more affection, as it did not fit in with the templates. Of course he is a musician, and it is normal for musicians to dress a bit extravagantly. Overall, however, he matched the required style, only changing one small detail.

Despite the fact that all styles and fashions are also clichés we should still follow fashion, bringing something of ourselves to it.

So that we feel confident and so those around us would take us seriously, let's work on our wardrobe a little.

These are the six most widely adopted styles:

Classic

Sporty

Romantic

Cultural

Retro

Casual

There are also four emotional states:

Fading out

Rebirth

Creativity

Withering away

which are linked to the four seasons — winter, spring, summer, and autumn.

We choose the most appropriate style for each event, for each meeting. We add a small, but at first glance indiscernible detail from our own selves — a little emotional note, which corresponds to one or another of the emotional states, or to the time of year.

EXERCISE 5 ●

Prepare your video camera or smartphone: Both your text, and your outfit, where possible, need to be among the six listed styles; together with a recording of a composition of Antonio Vivaldi's 'The Four Seasons.'

Try to dress in a way that corresponds to each style in turn. I would advise starting with the classical style and add to your outfit a small, almost indiscernible detail in line with that season. This could be a brooch, a badge, a scarf and so on. Just find your detail and don't trust the first idea that comes into your head.

In order to create the corresponding atmosphere switch on the recording of 'The Four Seasons,' for example 'Winter.' Are you ready? If you are then switch on the video camera or smartphone, stand at a distance of approximately three steps away from the camera, so that you fill the frame.

If you are ready, then start to dance to Vivaldi's music. Your movements should be your own, just get a feel for the music. With the help of this music, enter into the atmosphere of this season. Move for one and a half minutes.

Stop, and let the music keep playing, start to read your text in the spirit of that specific time of year. That is to say, if it is winter then imagine yourself in that atmosphere, imagine snow or a blizzard around you, and if it is spring then imagine the birds singing, and the freshness. If the season is autumn, then imagine the rain, and if it is summer then the scalding sun and heat.

Recite your text from this atmosphere and try to gesticulate. Add only hand movements to make it more convincing. Don't, however, be overzealous: I often find myself thinking that people, when they are recording vlogs, gesticulate deliberately in front of the camera, but they don't do it theatrically enough, so that their hands and their words move separately from one another. It should all look natural.

Do this exercise for each of the four seasons, and for each of the six styles. Watch the video recording. Analyze which of the styles you felt most comfortable in. Don't forget to accept yourself for who you are. For this to happen do not take yourself and your dance, costume, or mannerisms too seriously. At that moment be your own director, and not an artiste. Improve on what you like about your performance and take out what you don't like.

CHAPTER 8

The King of The Absurd

In the seventh chapter we examined the components of the character we are creating, as well as the nature of our performance.

In the eighth chapter you will meet my second teacher, the King of the Absurd, and you will be convinced that two plus two does not always equal four. Sometimes it equals five, sometimes three, and sometimes nothing at all.

DON QUIXOTE

The King of the Absurd did not look at us during our classes. He looked out of the window. Cars passed by, and buses: rain fell, snow, and the sun shone. The seasons passed and he would just continue to look out of the window, as though he never went home, turning his back on us.

We were students at the clowning institute in Moscow, and we would show him our endless homework in the form of sketches and observations of people and of animals.

As he continued to look out of the huge window the King of the Absurd mumbled:

'It's not funny, it's tasteless, talentless, and uninspired.'

Once I showed him some study or other. Again, not tearing his gaze away from the window, he suddenly asked:

'Do you know what time the train to Kharkov leaves from the Kursk station?'

'At 22:00 hrs,' I answered.

'You have time to buy a ticket for that train and go home. Go into business, get married, you have good teeth, free the public from the misery of having to look at you.'

My second teacher the King of the Absurd was himself an example of the absurd. He was tall and thin, he had a beard and a moustache and he fought imaginary enemies, problems that did not exist. He looked like Don Quixote. That was the nickname we gave him — Don Quixote. Funny things were always happening to him and around him.

Opposite the building in Moscow's Izmailova where I studied at the clowning institute was a delicatessen. Once after lessons the King of the Absurd bought a dozen fresh turkey cutlets from there. We traveled with him to his dacha, where he organized a modest party.

As he walked up to his 'Lada' car a pigeon that had been sitting on a branch relieved itself on his elegant jacket. Outraged, the King placed the bag with the cutlets on the driver's seat and started to wipe his jacket with a paper towel.

One minute later he, having forgotten about the cutlets, and outraged at the pigeon, sat behind the wheel, straight onto the bag, which he had not noticed at all. I had also not noticed it. All the way there he was telling us that he had not been to his dacha for a month, as he had not had a spare tire and he was afraid of getting a puncture. The day before, however, he had somehow been able to get hold of a spare and now he could go wherever he wanted. Suddenly his car started to drift to the right. The King of the Absurd stopped on the highway to Podmoskovye and got out to check his tire, some time later he returned and sat silently behind the wheel.

This time I noticed that he had sat on his own cutlets. I wanted to tell him about this, but I held my silence, since the King was obviously distressed about something and was deeply immersed in his own thoughts.

'This tire hates me,' murmured the King quietly under his beard.

I got out to see what had happened. The back wheel was destroyed. We grabbed the jack and the spare tire and changed the wheel. The King, again not noticing the cutlets, sat on them. I saw this but again I was unable to warn him. The King was constantly saying, without letting me get a word in: 'I don't like traveling on a spare tire. It's very dangerous, traveling without a spare. It always happens to me. Even if I took 2, or 3, or 15 spare tires with me they would all get a puncture.'

We had hardly traveled a kilometre and again the car began to drift to the right. The King stopped and got out of the car. The spare was also destroyed. The King got back into the car and sat on his cutlets, at last he noticed this and pulled the bag out from under him. Having carefully examined what was left of the turkey cutlets, he said sadly: 'I told you today we would be left without a spare, and without cutlets.'

Don Quixote, who was always dressed in a wonderful, elegant suit, was very serious, he was even, like the White Clown, pompous, and carried an air of importance. When he came into the classroom it seemed like the minister for economics himself was walking into the classroom. He was very funny with his pomposity, and sometimes, like Don Quixote, he was deplorably absurd.

On one occasion two students showed him their sketch, the 'Car' using two chairs. The King of the Absurd seized upon the student who was playing the role of the driver: 'And who drives like that?' He grabbed his enormous teaching desk, put it in the middle of the room, hoisted two chairs onto the table and sat in the improvised driver's seat. He picked up a hoop that served as a wheel and began to demonstrate how this car needs to be driven, repeating:

'You need to do it in such a way that the public believes that you are driving a car. The public should sense your car and even the bad roads. You should be shaken around all the time.'

The King began to throw himself around and it was really funny. The chair began to slowly move towards the edge of the table as a result of this shaking. The King of the Absurd was just about to fall.

We students saw this but we could not say anything to the King, since he at that time really was driving a car and his thoughts were elsewhere. Maybe he was in the Caucasus Mountains or perhaps in the forests of Siberia.

Meanwhile the chair reached the edge of the table and the two-meter tall King fell onto the floor in his chair. A silence hung over the room. After a few moments the King jumped to his feet, contented, and shouted:

'Did you see that: that is how to drive a car and fall. You talentless lot!'

Before I continue to tell you about the King of the Absurd, however, I will tell you about the road that led me to my second teacher.

THE CENTRAL ASIAN STORIES

Getting into the Moscow clowning studio under the All-Union directorate for the preparation of new programmes, attractions, and acts, which was based in Izmailova, was unbelievably difficult. The studio was considered the best higher education institute of its kind in the Soviet Union.

In the spring of 1988 the all-union competition for a place at this studio was announced, and I arrived to enroll along with my friend and my first clowning partner, Knyaz Melik Ter-Compassion.

Knyaz Ter- Compassion was Armenian, but was born in Azerbaijan in the city of Kirovobad (now Ganja). His large family lived there.

We remain friends to this day. Empathy often hides behind what seems like a rugged nature. It is for this reason that I gave him that name. He is not one to walk past when another person is suffering. If you fall, Knyaz will pick you up without fail, he will help you, make any necessary calls, feed you and so on.[15]

When my friend was 14 years old, his father brought him to Kharkov to study as a plumber and gas welder at the professional technical college No. 14. That was where I met him, and we became friends at rehearsals for my first teacher, the King of Fate.

By the time the entrance exams for the clowning institute came around, we had lost our clowning talents. We had lost them at the philharmonic halls where we had been working since we were 16, in 1984. But we had a passion, a desire to become real clowns.

[15] Translator's note: in Russian the term 'sostradanie' from the name Knyaz Melik. Ter-Sostradanie means 'empathy'.

The last philharmonic hall Knyaz and I performed in was located in Uzbekistan in the city of Andizhan. The public did not laugh. 'Play the music louder so the reaction of the crowd cannot be heard, and if the public don't laugh they can at least listen to the music,' our director, administrator, cashier, leader and artiste of an original genre Iban Ibanovna Swift, who had dreamed of 'working the big time,' advised us. I did not clarify what that meant, but I noticed that almost all the employees of the circuses that performed on stage at the regional philharmonics in the Soviet Union, from the artistes to the administrators, dreamed of working the big time, using this expression like it was something superfluous, where they needed to use it and where they didn't.

The pervasive atmosphere in the circus brigades under the Soviet regional philharmonic halls was horrible. More often than not the artistes who worked there were either very old, or very young, or had not been successful. Almost always the administrators were, in one way or another, crooks who had dreamed of earning money out of the confusion of Soviet life.

I will tell a few stories of what happened at the regional philharmonic halls of Central Asia so that the reader understands the atmosphere in which we worked.

BURNING HEARTS

Usually a few days prior to the arrival of our circus brigade at any district center, such as Karkasa in the Andizhan region for example, our administrator Ibana Ibanovna Swift would arrive along with her driver, Yuriy Elonovich Musk. As you have already realized, what lies behind these names is a generalized image of all Soviet circus brigade administrators and their drivers.

Comparing our driver to Elon Musk at first glance does not ring true, as he is a rich inventor of the technology of the future, and not a slacker without any professional skills. Our Yuriy Elonovich Musk was not a slacker without any professional skills either. He was an engineer, and an inventor, maybe not of space ships that are ready to set off on a seven-month mission to Mars, or of electric battery-powered cars, or of super high-speed tunnels for cars under Los Angeles and so on, but just simple everyday electrical goods that were ready to comfort a great many people here on Earth. Unfortunately, however, in the Soviet Union engineers and inventors were not valued. Therefore our Musk worked officially as a driver for a circus brigade.

He really was a creative person. Over the entire course of our tour around Kazakhstan, Yuriy Elonovich was always inventing things. From an electric kettle, which boiled our water with the help of razor blades, to the springs for the heaters, which kept us warm in the cold hotels of northern Kazakhstan.

He even invented components for our GAZ-24 vehicle. After all, purchasing a new component in the endless steppes of Soviet Kazakhstan was impossible. There in Kazkahstan, as in the Soviet city of Kharkov, in a more moderate continental climate in the northern tracts of the European part of the country, these components were in very short supply.

Yes, our Yuriy Elonovich was not a rich man in a financial sense, he never made it onto the top ten of the Forbes list, not even in the bottom ten, but he had a kind and understanding heart. If a list was published of similar qualities, Yuriy Elonovich would be right up there in the top ten.

Therefore, there was only one aim of this couple's arrival at the regional center: they would hang old posters of the Great Moscow circus on bus stops, in shops, and at the post office.

Musk would carefully cut around the dates of the tours, or would glue new dates onto them.

The posters promised wild animals, acrobats riding camels, jugglers, aerial gymnasts, illusionary tricks, and funny clowns.

Three days later and three hours before the performance, a 'Volga' service vehicle would arrive at the palace of culture, and the five of us would get out: Knyaz and I, our Yuriy Elonovich Musk, who was always battling his broken down vehicle, he a lighting technician and a sound technician.

Ibana Ibanovna Swift would also get out of the car, she was the administrator, and the ticket seller. She was also the ringleader of the show with her silly verses, and she was an artiste of an original genre with her own short act with hula-hoops, and she was the trainer of the four doves that were constantly tired from their traveling.

The last to get out of the car, as a National Artiste of the Uzbek Soviet Socialist Republic, was Khashira Kazbek, and she was the usher, and an artiste with her own short act entitled 'The Contortionist and the Rose' (although in view of her advanced years she did not perform this act every time). On the other hand, even with a temperature, she would work her shows, and specifically she would perform an illusionary trick called 'The Flowers of the East,' with which we would always end our show.

We would take a cage with four doves from out of the boot of the 'Volga,' along with the promised wild animals and camels, the hula-hoops, a suitcase with the props for the shows, a suitcase with our clowns' belongings, a table for the 'Contortionist,' an amplifier and two speakers.

Yury Elonovich would uncoil the equipment. The very first thing he did would be to connect the microphone. The sound was like the No. 34 bus in the city of Kharkov when the driver is announcing the stops. 'One, two, three, setting up the equipment...' Musk would repeat this text several times, lowering and raising his voice. I never heard any variation in this.

After checking that he had done everything he could with the sound, Yuriy Elonovich would set about the lighting. The quality of the lighting more often than not corresponded to that of the sound. A pair of studio lighting boards hanging to the left and right and a cinema projector without a reel was all that we had at our disposal. There was exactly a meter from the screen down to the floor that was not lit up, and in the end we, as artistes, ended up being only half illuminated.

Ibana Ibanovna sat in the box office to sell tickets. Exactly one hour before the performance Khashira would stand at the entrance checking the tickets. At that same time my partner would connect the iron to the mains, but this was not to iron our suits.

The audience would gradually fill the auditorium. Around 50 minutes before the performance I would approach Khashira Kazbek. Khashira was still working as an usher, and she would not leave what she was doing. She was just collecting tickets, and when I approached her she would hand me the crumpled bunch of tickets.

I would take them backstage where Knyaz would iron each ticket with a hot iron, and the ironed tickets would be taken to Ibana Ibanovna in the box office so she could sell them a second time.

This combination was called the 'turnstyle.' As you have already guessed, having sold the tickets a second time they would write in the reports that the audience did not turn up, even though after the posters we put up we had full houses.

I don't know why my partner and I did that. Iban and Khashira were on the payroll, but we were not paid anything, only our daily subsistence and seven rubles, our fee for the performance.

The show would begin at exactly 19:05 hrs, not because we would take an 'academic' five minutes, but because Ibana Ibanovna closed the box office at 19:00 hrs and needed five minutes to throw off her coat and colour her lips.

Yuriy Elonovich Musk would hand a grey plastic microphone to her that had a horrible sound. Ibana Ibanovna with a little skip would jump on stage in such a way that her dress, which was covered in glistening sequins, would also jump around, revealing her toned legs. Once she was in the middle of the stage, Swift would fervently read the following lines:

'Good evening, young people!
Good day, burning hearts!
We will not be looking at your passports,
There's no end to our youth.'

Then she would say something else and then at last she would announce us.

Knyaz and I would come out onto the stage, made-up and decked out. Thank God, I have forgotten what it was we actually did.

Khashira Kazbek at this time, and almost right up until her first act 'The Contortionist and the Rose,' stood like a sentry at the entrance and would not let anyone in without a ticket. She would have to sell the crumpled tickets that had not been ironed to those who were late.

In the next act, without any announcement, Ibana Swift would jump out with her hula-hoops and would begin to rotate them as fast as she could. Sometimes she would choke, most likely because she smoked heavily.

Once in the car when we were returning to the hotel after our show, Ibana told us that she performed her act with the hula-hoops in Stanislavskiy's style. She even told us that she had a higher purpose in her act. She explained that each hoop was not a hoop at all, but an admirer that had won her over.

According to Ibana the act consisted of her spinning everyone around her and dominating everyone, leaving herself as 'the last,' to spin around — as if she were in a 'barrel' — joining with her admirer in ecstasy. In this case the 'barrel' was the hula-hoops connected on four sides by twine.

This was maybe how it looked in her youth, but Ibana was already advancing in years, she smoked heavily, and would barely spin the hoops. It could hardly be called ecstasy.

Five minutes before her entrance Khashira would leave her position at the door, run backstage, throw off her night gown, take off her camel hair belt that was coiled around her waist, and would nervously warm up her back. Ibana would put out her table and announce her.

After her performance Khashira would put on her camel hair belt as she was walking, throw on her hat, and would again run to the entrance to check tickets. After selling a few more tickets, and prior to her illusionist show, she would return backstage, change into her evening dress, cover her face in a mysterious black mask, and after that, as Ibana was again announcing her, Khashira Kazkbek would again appear on stage to the sound of strange music, the gaze of a spotlight on her waist and a fan in her hand.

She would do a couple of tricks involving rings, scarves, and balls. There were times when Kazbek would stop her act to ask Yuriy Elonovich to stop the music. This happened because Khashira would suddenly notice that people were coming into the hall without tickets.

She would take the microphone, and, addressing those who had just come into the hall in Uzbek, would ask them to leave. Once they had obeyed her and left, she would say in Russian: 'No conscience: music maestro please!'

Yuriy Elonovich Musk would again play the recording.

HUNTING

Right at the start of our professional clowning career we worked at the Aktyubinsk regional philharmonic in Kazakhstan. Once, we arrived into a district where people were suffering acutely from hunger. This town was called Krasnoe. There was no food in this town. The windows of the food shops were decorated only with canned fish, which it was impossible to buy: they would only be distributed to those who showed their Veteran of labour or Veteran of the Great Patriotic War cards.

Since none of us were veterans of labour, even less of the war, we would come back to the hotel hungry after the show. We started to think of where we might find food. Knyaz Ter--Compassion found from somewhere a sack and a torch, he handed these things to me and said, 'We are going up into the loft to look for food — we are after doves.

The doves would be sleeping now; what is key now is that we act quickly. As soon as you see a dove, shine the torch right into their eyes before they realize what is going on, and I will grab them and chuck them in the sack.'

We climbed up to the loft. There were a lot of doves there. Knyaz Ter-Compassion said that we needed ten doves, two each for all of us.

'Are you ready?' he asked me in a whisper, so as not to scare the birds.

'I am ready.'

'Switch on!'

I shone the torch on the first dove. Knyaz Melik Ter-Compassion grabbed the dove with his hands, squeezed its head between his index and middle fingers, and in a single sharp movement yanked it towards him in such a way, that the dove's head would be in his right hand, and the body in his left.

'Move the sack up.'

I moved the sack and Knyaz chucked the beheaded body of the dove into it.

To say I was shocked would be to say nothing. I had thought Knyaz would just chuck the doves into the sack. What I did not know, however, was that he would tear a dove's head off — a dove, a symbol of peace, as in the paintings of Pablo Picasso.

'Are you ready?' whispered Melik Ter-Compassion, interrupting my thoughts about the doves, the works of art dedicated to them, and that in religion these birds symbolize the Holy Spirit.

'I'm ready,' I said gingerly, without looking at the process of decapitation.

This was how we got hold of ten doves for ourselves, and each worker at the palace of culture had two doves.

Khashira plucked them. Yuriy Elonovich put together a water heater made from two razor blades and matches and procured a huge saucepan, we got hold of some macaroni from somebody and someone else had onions and carrots. Ibana Ibanovna brought vanilla grass. We made a delicious soup. Knyaz and I were the heroes of that evening.

THE LAST STRAW

We had already thought about giving up our work for the philharmonic halls. The last straw was the mishap that occurred in Uzbekistan in the town of Andizhan. Our posters attracted a capacity crowd, but the show clearly did not meet with their expectations of quality.

In the front row sat three brightly dressed Aqsaqals with their white beards and white turbans. It was as though they were asleep but with their eyes open. They did not react to us at all, they did not clap, or laugh, they did not express any emotions right up until the very mid-point of the show.

Suddenly, these three old men woke up, looked at each other and muttered something to themselves under their breath in Uzbek. They then left the hall in an organized manner along with dozens of young teenagers and younger children, and then just five minutes later they returned. Knyaz and I were at that moment performing the clowning act 'The Apple,' which we hated. Suddenly clods of mud came flying towards us.

Thinking that this was the public's reaction to us as clowns, we quickly left the stage, to allow Khashira Kazbek with her 'Contortionist' act. They did not like her either — clods of mud came flying her way as well. It was a little more difficult for Khashira to leave the stage, since she was already in a pose on a table positioned at height and was bent double.

Summoning up her courage, Khashira performed her trick to the end. She stopped the music, grabbed the microphone and began to educate the audience in Uzbek.

The public calmed down, but three minutes later the three Aqsaqals again mumbled something under their breath.

The clods of mud again appeared on the stage. The hall began to chant: 'Disgrace, disgrace, disgrace!' We could not continue with the show.

The public began to demand their money back, but soon discovered they had no tickets. A huge crowd gathered around the box office and Ibana Ibanovna Swift was forced to give whoever asked for it a refund.

I clearly had to change something in my career. I understood that I either had to study, or leave this profession. Somewhere in a newspaper I came across by chance an announcement that the Moscow All-Union directorate for the preparation of new programmes, shows and acts was announcing a competition for places on professional clowning courses. I understood that this was my chance.

How though could we find our way out of this miserable situation? After all, we had a contract with the Andizhan Philharmonic. We did not even have enough money for a return ticket.

I called my mum from a national telephone exchange and asked her to send a telegram to the director of the Andizhan Philharmonic, comrade Dzhelgasov:

> 'Circus clowns Knyaz Melik Ter-Compassion
> and Mikhail Usov return to Moscow urgently 25
> April, participation International Festival Paris.'

We were summoned to Andizhan, to the office of the Director of the Philharmonic, comrade Dzhelgasov. He showed us the telegram and in an eastern accent he said: 'This is a great honour for you and for our Philharmonic. Congratulations!'

The Philharmonic bought our airline tickets and sent us to Moscow.

This was only possible in the Soviet Union — that a telegram from my mum Baroness Oberfeldt in Kharkov was mistaken for an invitation from the International Festival in Paris.

'If you become famous, tell them about me'

So there we were in Moscow. The competition for the clowning studio was huge, almost 30 people for every place. Young and entertaining people arrived from all across the Soviet Union.

Knyaz and I just performed that same clowning act. The Apple,' and fell flat on our face. By the time of our enrollment the clowning act had turned into a cliché, there was no life left in it.

We were rejected in the third round. They said of me that I lacked a sense of rhythm. We, however, did not give up and we decided to enroll at the Moscow circus college. Knyaz found the King of the Absurd somewhere in Moscow and requested his help in preparing for the exams.

I prepared for them myself, and again I was rejected in the third round. This time they said that I had bulgy eyes, and that this is an affliction for a clown. The desperation that I experienced is hard to describe.

My partner, who was trained by the King of the Absurd, was successful in the competition and was enrolled at the Moscow circus college in the clowning faculty.

I was forced to return to Kharkov. On my bed for two months, I looked at the ceiling, studying its cracks. It seemed to me that I was intimately acquainted with all the spiders on the ceiling and with the flies that they caught in their webs.

Even up until now I still cannot imagine myself living in Kharkov.

Suddenly the phone rang, and it was my friend Knyaz, my partner, who had been a student of the Moscow circus college for a month by that time. He told me that one student had been expelled from the clowning studio in Izmailova.

The examination commission back in the summer had not appreciated that he was not well and, more to the point, he was a schizophrenic, but it was this that had more than likely made him very funny. When the lessons began this came to light, and he was expelled for health reasons.

Knyaz Melik Ter- Compassion told me that a free place had come up in the studio as a result and that this was my chance: 'Come to Moscow straight away. I have agreed things with Don Quixote (with the King of the Absurd). He will train you. Each lesson costs ten rubles. You will need to have ten lessons. Don Quixote asked me to tell you to buy a real clown costume. You will enroll in that costume.'

My mum had 159 rubles in her savings account. In order that the account was not closed she withdrew 156 rubles. This was the last of our family's money.

On that day at the second hand store we found an almost new and relatively cheap costume. It cost 15 rubles. That evening I rushed to Moscow in a third class sleeper carriage with a ticket that cost 10 rubles.

Straight from the station I set off to meet the King of the Absurd on Frunzenskaya embankment. Instead of 'Hello!' he said to me: 'If you become famous — tell them about me, but if you're a loser, forget about me.'

He took me to a small TV room. There someone, evidently a television technician, was carrying a television. Back then they were still Soviet valve-operated televisions.

The King of the Absurd introduced me to the television technician as an artiste of the Maly Theatre. Since we were, allegedly, preparing a show for the Maly Theatre, we were not to be disturbed. The television technician whispered a promise not to disturb us.

The King of the Absurd, with a serious look on his face, told me that the colour contrast had gone in the television. After sitting me down in a chair, he began to pace back and forth, trying to dissuade me from enrolling at the clowning studio. I only recall fragments from this first introductory conversation.

'The circus is hellishly hard work. None of it is easy. Why do you need all that? You have good teeth, it would be better to find yourself some foreign girl, make her fall in love with you and get married.'

Once he could see that his attempts to convince me were not working, he began to describe the profession of being a clown:

'Being a clown — is not a profession — it's a way of life. Farada (Semyon Farada, a famous Soviet comic actor) once told me that he knows how to fall in a funny way. I looked at Farada and said: 'But I know how to get up in a funny way.'

Suddenly a little girl ran into the room wearing glasses, with long pigtails. She was eight years old. She cried out:

'Papa, papa!..'

'Vera, my daughter, don't disturb us! I have an artiste with me from the Maly Theatre,' he gestured towards me and the television technician with an air of importance, 'we are rehearsing! Where is your mum?!'

He asked me to change into my costume. On seeing me in my costume, he adjusted the hair on my head and said that in this costume I looked like Sergey Esenin, so we would prepare his 'Song About a Dog' for the exams.

At some point the television technician said:

'Is this going to the Maly Theatre or staying here....Have you got a cloth?'

The King of the Absurd handed over a cloth fastidiously:

'Holy cow, why did you call me?'

The television technician scraped the dirt off the television screen with a damp cloth — there were spatters of sweet tea, or jam, or some sort of syrup, which had plastered the entire surface of the television screen. The layer of dirt and dust was a centimeter thick.

'Vera, where is your mum?' the King of the Absurd cried out.

The technician switched on the television...the picture was excellent. The television was showing the Semyon Farada film 'The Conjurers.'

LESSON 6 — OR
2+2 = 5, AND SOMETIMES 3, AND OCCASIONALLY 0

The King of the Absurd began to prepare me for the exam. This preparation took two weeks. As I mentioned above, each lesson cost 10 rubles, which in the Soviet Union was a large amount of money.

At the sixth lesson, when I rang the bell for his flat on Frunzenskaya, the King of the Absurd was in no hurry to respond. Some time later the door opened on the chain.

He asked:

'Have you brought the money?'

'I have.'

'Well, give it here.'

I reached into my pocket for the ten rubles. He stretched out his long dry arm through the opening that had appeared in the door, took the money and said: 'The lesson is over.'

The King of the Absurd slammed the door right in my face. I was left standing there thinking that this was a joke. I waited for him to open the door again so he could teach me. Moreover, at the previous lesson number 5, he had told me that for a clown sometimes two plus two does not equal four. Sometimes it equals three, and occasionally nothing at all.

The door did not open again... I walked around near his flat for a while and then I went back and rang the doorbell again. Nobody opened the door. I went home, offended and disgruntled. The following day I again went back for lesson number 7. He opened the door, and he was in a good mood, as though nothing had happened. We worked fruitfully. It was at that lesson that he said: 'Now in any unforeseen circumstances, in life or on stage, you will have that experience of lesson number six. You should understand this well, and more than that, it should become a part of you: for a clown, two plus two equals zero, sometimes three, sometimes five, and occasionally even four. When we are trying to line up a reprise, we intentionally break the rules — the public laugh at this and the next moment they will already be expecting us to break the rules again, and we cheat them and play by the rules. That way we will always be one step ahead of the public.'

The day of the exam went well enough. I was enrolled at the famous Moscow clowning studio as a student. In its time great masters such as Yuriy Nikulin and his clowning partner Mikhail Shuydin had graduated from this studio. This event changed my whole life.

Those ten unbelievable lessons by the King of the Absurd opened the door for me to the circus proper. In ten days I understood more than I had in my four years of 'professional activity' in the regional philharmonics.

The King of the Absurd would often tell me during our lessons:

'More than anything you should become an interesting person, someone it's good to have a beer with, and only then a clown.'

A CONTINUATION OF LESSON 6

Three years later I was very surprised when I saw my teacher, the King of the Absurd, in Moscow on stage at the Bolshoi concert hall in Izmailova. He was performing in a huge, famous hall before two thousand people.

One of the clowns had fallen ill and the King of the Absurd had been asked to replace him. My impressions of my teacher's clowning acts were, unfortunately, not so great. He had gone back on everything that he had taught us. He was tense, afraid, and unnatural. The public did not react to him at all. I admit that I was now disappointed with my King of the Absurd.

At the lessons he was for us the funniest and wisest clown. After his failure I understood that theory is one thing, and practice is quite another.

When you are on stage a thousand factors begin to come into play, many of which are completely unpredictable, and you have to prepare for them in a certain way. You have to find and formulate your relationship to everything in advance, whatever happens on stage.

As I went backstage to see my teacher, it was hard for me to find the words to say to him. He met me in the corridor. He did not wait for my compliments, on the contrary he uttered impatiently:

'What you saw tonight, that was my lesson number 6.'

Therefore, that's how it is with real teachers: whatever they do — there are always lessons, whether you assimilate them or not. Whether they are positive or negative.

The King of the Absurd taught me not to accept the world through a template, but to see the invisible and hear the inaudible.

CHAPTER 9

Charisma

In chapter eight, with the example of the King of the Absurd, we learned that not everything unfolds with the same logic as our minds dictate. We also learned that intentional use of the element of alogism in our performances makes them more colourful and memorable.

We will dedicate chapter nine to charisma.

We will try to define what charisma is and what it is composed of, as well as touching on the four centers of gravity in more detail.

THE TEMPLATE AND LOVE

There is no concise definition of the term 'charisma.' Some authors say that charisma cannot be studied; you have to be born with it. Others think that charisma can be developed and you only need approach this in the right way. On the Internet we can find an enormous number of questions on this subject. People either want to be, or to become, charismatic.

It seems to me that you really do have to be born with charisma. Furthermore, it strikes me that we are all born with charisma but in time our charisma, and along with it our individuality, accumulate templates through which we perceive the world. I have defined some of the most important aspects of this understanding for myself.

Charisma — is magic, which comes from the very depths of a person's soul. I have discovered that it is directly linked to the state of the Invisible Clown. If we are already in the state of the Invisible Clown, then even thoughts about our own charisma can dispel our wonderful state, along with that same charisma.

In the state of the Invisible Clown, questions no longer arise for us over whether we can become charismatic, or if we can develop that quality within us and win the love and respect of those around us. If we are already born with this quality, then all we need do is to free ourselves from our templates through which we perceive the world and ourselves.

What you look like or how old you are is not important here. What is important is to remain yourself and not to structure your life according to a template, perform to a template, build the character of your persona around a template, and structure the nature of what you do around a template.

Anywhere there is a template there is no charisma. Anywhere there is a template there is no love, and it's indeed the case that wherever there is a template there is no life. It's all very simple: a template — represents death, love — represents life.

We are all so different that, having found differentiation within ourselves, we perceive it as an idiosyncrasy. We are afraid of appearing idiosyncratic. We suppress these manifestations deep within us. To be like everyone else means to be modest, to go with the flow, and not put our heads above the parapet.

However, charisma is the quality of a leader, and to be a leader is not to be just one of the herd, but to lead the herd from the front. If not leading the herd from the front, then staying true to who we are. This is what it is to 'be unique.'

It is wonderful if there is a modicum of idiosyncrasy in the character you are planning to adopt, and moreover, there is an element of your charisma in that same idiosyncrasy.

All the clowns that I know find some idiosyncrasy in the character they create, and an obvious level of success follows for those who do not copy the ideas of others, which have already become templates, but find something of their own within themselves.

Confirmation of this can be found in other professions, which in one way or another involve dealing with the public. Even in the profession of a president.

Everyone has heard the words of the 40th President of the United States, Ronald Reagan, after his attempted assassination. When his wife Nancy came to the hospital where the operation was due to be carried out, he smiled and said: 'Honey, I forgot to duck.' The president continued with his witty remarks even after the operation.[16]

But after all, is this not an element of charisma? Is it not a clown's logic? A politician makes bold use of this and becomes a favourite.

Do not be afraid of appearing funny and idiosyncratic, this sets you apart from other people and makes them remember you. On the contrary, be afraid of behaving in the 'correct' way.

Our idiosyncrasies represent our child that is still there deep down inside of us, yearning and waiting for its time to appear.

[16] https://www.bbc.com/russian/international/2011/03/110330_reagan_attempt_anniversary

Jesus says:

'Be as children.'[17]

For me this means opening ourselves up again and finding in ourselves something childlike. The child in you wants to manifest itself, wallow around like an idiot, cry out loud, jump up and down, and so on.

When the acrobats — former sportsmen — come to Cirque du Soleil, they are extraordinarily reserved and tense. Acrobats only see the gymnastic apparatus in their sport. They approach, perform their combination of moves, and then leave. It's all very serious and there are no emotions involved. The circus deliberately gives them specific sets of exercises to do so that the acrobats become artistes. The directors and choreographers work with them to reawaken the child in them.

If you are not an acrobat who has been hired by Cirque du Soleil, or you are not a clown, or an artiste, how can you reawaken the child in you? We are so shackled in life by the confines of society's standards of behaviour that when we go beyond these standards, our minds automatically engage and our internal censor is activated, saying: 'Don't do that. What would people think about me?' Or: 'how old are you?' and so on and so on.

Reawakening your inner child is a manifestation of inner freedom.

Something happened to the very famous clown Oleg Popov, after which he became famous all over the world. Once the Soviet circus was on tour in Belgium, and Queen Fabio de Mora y Aragón invited some of the Soviet artistes and administrators to her palace for a reception. Either out of ignorance or by

[17] The Gospel of Matthew, 18:3 Ter-Sostradanie means 'empathy.'

intention Oleg Popov drank some water from a bowl that was intended for washing the guests' hands. Naturally the queen thought that the 'Russian' was doing this on purpose because he was a clown, a naïve clown. The Queen of Belgium named Popov 'the Sunshine Clown,' and it was this strange incident that made him famous the world over.[18]

Or another example, Vladimir Ivanovich Kremena, a Soviet clown who was famous for starring in a number of films. Once we were walking along the street in the city of Vyatka from the hotel to the circus. A man was walking towards us with a disheveled appearance and a haggard face, and, judging by his breath, he was far from sober.

Kremena stopped and spoke to him:

'Soldier..'

As he drew level with us the passer-by looked at Vladimir Ivanovich and in his tired, drunken eyes a question had formed:

'What?'

Kremena stared at him:

'Soldier, are you going to throw a grenade for me?'

'Throw…'

Vladimir Ivanovich welled up. He took off the enormous gilded watch he wore on his wrist, held it out to the drunken man, and added:

'Wear this, it's a commander's watch…'

The 'soldier' remained where he was, standing stock still, and we continued to the circus. There, Kremena pulled a new watch out of a small cardboard box that contained dozens of these same watches, put it on his wrist and wore it until he met the next soldier.

---

[18] Oleg Popov. The circus remained, the clown left. – https://tvkultura.ru/article/show/article_id/19021/

'You half-wit, nobody will fall in love with you. Never bring your girl along to one of your shows,' Kremena once said to me after I had returned to the dressing room from make-up. It was his biggest compliment to me. I served my apprenticeship with him, and he called me to come out on stage with just one reprise.

As I did not have any other performances at this arena, I had to trim my character down to a point so as to concentrate, make it more definitive, and therefore funnier. The public did laugh as a result of my concentration, and the act went down very well.

In Paris I saw a homeless person with an enormous grey sack on his back and wearing huge boots like those of a clown, with trousers that were also the wrong size and a piece of cable instead of a belt. He was walking down the very long street called the Elysian Fields among the autumnal, almost bare trees. Above him, like a gigantic storm cloud, a flock of street pigeons circled. They would perch on his head, shoulders, and on his sack. Occasionally this man would chase away the pigeons that perched on him with his right hand, as if they were flies, but nevertheless they would perch all over this strange man's body. He just carried on walking and walking.

You could see this man's entire life history, his loneliness. It was more than likely that apart from these birds, this man had no friends left, nor anyone to talk to. It was impossible to take my gaze away from this street show. I watched, I watched as this surprising man walked away until he became no more than a dot and then disappeared completely, along with his load and all his birds.

A child lives inside a clown that helps their character to be spontaneous.

A child lives inside each and every one of us. If we are able to reach our inner child, it means that we can reach the inner child of our viewer.

At one point our parents and our society helped us to become adults.

Now we, as clowns, are helping adults become children again.

LESSON 7 — THE IDIOSYNCRASY IN THE CHARACTER THAT YOU ARE CREATING

In order to reawaken your inner child, as well as overcome your stage fright and doubts, it is better to know yourself, and your limitations. I suggest going out onto the street of a bustling city and spoiling yourself a little. In this lesson we will need to perform three exercises. You will need a video camera or a smartphone (although I am not suggesting you film each of the exercises). Also, prepare white post-it notes, or pieces of blank white paper of any size.

EXERCISE 6 ●

Thanks to this exercise, called 'Stop,' you will understand that a pause is part of movement, and you will be able to break your routine and delve deep inside yourself, despite your external circumstances. Dress as you did for the last exercise, in a specific way that is the most comfortable style for you. Go out onto the busiest street where you live. Choose a location on this street with the most number of people walking in one direction. Stop for five minutes and do not move. Take in the sounds of the city, the sounds of the footsteps of the people walking past. Stop your thoughts. Let this be your small meditation in the busiest place. As with the first exercise, picture yourself sticking imaginary post-it notes on the back of a chair, which relate to your name. Now in this, your total inner silence, your emptiness, and in spite of the numbers of people all rushing somewhere, no less than three minutes after you stopped, lift your right foot two to three centimeters off the ground in such a way that nobody can see it. Now, with your leg raised up, read that text again from memory.

EXERCISE 7 ●

This exercise, called 'Animation,' will help you build up confidence in yourself, speak to other people easily, become well-connected, and open up new possibilities, as well as interact with the public directly. Take your post-it notes and blank pieces of white paper. Go out onto a busy street, hand these pieces of paper out to people. If people ask you what it is you are advertising, say: 'I am advertising emptiness.' Try without forcing anything to exchange a few sentences with people. If you are successful, engage in conversation.

EXERCISE 8 ●

This exercise, called 'Shadow,' will help you to keep your goal in mind, which only you can know, under any circumstances. Go out onto the street. Imagine that you have ended up in a city of shadows. Focus your attention just on the shadows. Set up the video camera. Start to walk, scrutinizing only the shadows, paying particular attention to yours. Start to film just your shadow on the video camera and the way it interacts with other shadows. You will see that other shadows will encroach on yours, that your shadow will traverse the shadow of a car and so on. This exercise can be done for 10-20 minutes. It will reawaken your inner child.

I did not want in this book to touch on performance techniques, but I really cannot avoid this. Without knowing them you cannot find your own image or character.

Let's run through some of them.

'A smile is a weapon for an actor,' the great director Georgiy Tovstonogov was fond of saying. This same rule applies to any performer. For a clown a smile, moreover, is heavy artillery. It is loaded. You don't have to smile very often but at the right time. Otherwise, we will be firing this weapon in vain.

Find a few places in your performance when you need to smile. They don't need to be many, no more than three. When you have to smile for real, gift your smile to the public.

Make-up and costume — all these are attributes of the character image, and although they are important, it is more important to perform on the basis of your inner experience: it is from this inner experience that an interesting character is born, and along with it your make-up and costume.

Each one of us is unique, therefore it is not easy — and, at the same time, very easy — to find your own image, or, if you like, your own identity, its shades, nuances, weaknesses, habits, and trivialities, to be yourself. Different schools of philosophy say different things about the uniqueness of the individual. This uniqueness in individuals is confirmed afresh when observing people. It is true that it is always linked to a person's consciousness. The more conscious a person is, the more unique they are.

It is worth developing a habit of observing yourself, other people, and life all the time and everywhere you go, in different situations. For example, with the help of observations I discovered that every human being is like an animal. This also helps to find your image, to understand which animal the character you are creating resembles.

It is important to know how to manage your center of gravity. Where an individual performer's center of gravity is depends on the character of their persona.

There are five main centers of gravity.

The first of these is found in the tailbone (on a material or an instinctive level).

The second is found in the legs, and more specifically in the calves (on a kinetic level).

The third is found close to the solar plexus (on an emotional level).

The fourth is found in the neck (on an intellectual level).

The fifth center can be found between your eyebrows — this is a higher level, our Invisible Clown.

If you need to play the role of a monster, villain, alcoholic, or an animal, try to shift your center of gravity to your tailbone. Your shoulders will move inwards. You will look down. You know, for example, that a pig always looks down and never upwards or up to the sky. Try to create the image of a pig that has realized that they are a pig and does not want to be anything but a pig. They will try to look up, but they will not be able to do this, but maybe just once. This is an example of how to give HOPE to your personality. Hope is another level in the character of your personality. The point being that there are levels within the character of your hero. You can fantasize over how low they can stoop and how high they can climb, where their boundaries are. These experiments demonstrate the scale and relativity of your personality.

If you need an image of an emotional person, open out your shoulders and breathe.

If you need to portray an intellectual, your center of gravity should be in your neck. Your neck should be under considerable pressure from your head, heavy from the multitude of thoughts.

In different circumstances the center of gravity will change, and the so-called points will be added. If you are playing an alcoholic and the alcoholic suddenly takes offence, your center of gravity will remain in your tailbone, but other points will be added in both ears. Let's imagine we have two big red ears like those of an elephant, and now let's try and send our energy into them. The energy would be divided between our tailbone and our two ears. Another analogy: if you need to play an intellectual but very inquisitive person who is always sniffing everything out, you can try to distribute the energy between your neck and the tip of your nose.

You can experiment with this at home or on the street, try to shift your center of gravity to your ears. Tailbone..., the tip of your nose, ...back of the neck...., the small toe on your left leg, and so on. You don't need a theatre or a hall of mirrors for these exercises. Try to do them in the metro, at the post office, at the bank or at the supermarket. Nobody need guess what you are doing. On the contrary, if people see what you are doing it means there is something wrong. Just do this for yourself. Only you will know what is happening.

After analyzing the ideas that are packed into different clowning acts, I identified four notional levels in comedic performances. Subsequently, and completely unexpectedly for myself, I saw that these same four levels encompass works in any art form.

1. The Kinetic — Instinctive Level

This is a sufficiently superficial level, which touches upon the lowest human instincts. In other words, it could be said: humour for the sake of humour, to meet the needs of the public, vulgar jokes and so on. Although often funny, these performers are not remembered by the public and are not particularly valued, they do not touch their audience. Any gain they make is movement for the sake of movement. In the circus clowns like these often seek someone out in the audience and just laugh at this person. The public laughs themselves into stitches, but for the person they use, the experience is painful.

In ballet, there are cases where a dancer will perform unbelievable tricks, which do not have any specific aim. When the dancer does not carry their image within them, these are again tricks for the sake of tricks, just costumes and tricks.

In painting, when an artist shows us in a work how virtuoso their technique is, how they can bring out details, but they are not trying to convey an idea of any kind to us, then that painting will not give rise to any emotions.

In architecture it's the same: we can see a house as a house, when we look, for example, at the faceless Khrushchevka flats.

2. The Emotional Level

Interpersonal relationships lie at the heart of this level. In the circus a clown only instigates a reprise with public out of love.

For example, they take a flower and offer it to one of the ladies in the audience; they are play acting and demonstrating that they love them. If this is done in a way that is forced or overzealous then nobody will believe that clown.

In painting, the bright colours occasionally represent feelings for the sake of feelings. These creations, of course, touch our souls, but this is nevertheless a world of extreme emotions, and you can 'cry over them' to the end of your days.

If an opera singer is a bad actor, then no matter how powerful their voice is they will not be able to convey real emotion. They, for example, will overact and then it just becomes mundane, it just doesn't sound right, there's no 'in between.' It is impossible to hear a performance like that, it makes you wretch. Another extreme is if love and feelings are communicated directly. It is easy to see this in karaoke when professional artistes sing love songs. They put so much feeling into it.

This, however, not only relates to interpersonal relationships. It relates to extreme emotions towards anything that surrounds us. I saw in Germany a monument to a fireman, who had been burnt in a fire. Modern art. The fireman had suffered terrible burns, all his spine had been burnt right down to the bone; and in the same way a wolf howls at the moon, this poor fireman is screaming out in pain, their head raised up. It is impossible to look at the statue. It gives rise to way too many emotions and feelings. It conveys only pain and suffering, it's mundane. Therefore, you cannot feel sorry for the fireman, the statue, on the contrary, it conveys the opposite emotion.

3. The Intellectual Level

If we are to discuss the subject of presentations, then more often that not this is a speech that contains a lot of ideas, but is so boring to listen to that it is impossible to digest. Since our intellect works slowly, then the presentation itself will be slow. I know even some clowns who arrange everything carefully and work every joke, unfortunately however, this does not reach the public. This is because it is dry and very miscalculated.

In literature, ideas are encountered that are devoid of a joie de vivre. Such as truth, for example, which does not reach anyone and is as dry as dust, because it does not contain enough of a higher purpose.

4. The Higher Level

The higher level, or the level of the Invisible Clown, unites these three levels — the kinetic-instinctive level, the emotional level, and the intellectual level, and at the same time hovers above them all. You can do whatever you want to do at this higher level. If you are a clown, you could even take off your boxers, approach the object of your affections holding a bouquet of flowers and so on — it doesn't matter. Your entire performance will hang on a grandiose and large-scale idea, which would be important to, and understood by, the majority of people on Earth.

Great clowns such as Charlie Chaplin, Grok, Rivel, and Yengibarov are associated with this 'higher level'. As are the architectural works of art that I have already mentioned above, the Notre-Dame Cathedral in Paris, Chartres and Cologne Cathedrals, the Church of the Intercession on the Nerl.

In music, the 'St Matthew's Passion' and Bach's 'Mass in B Minor,' or the works of Vivaldi.

In painting: Rembrandt, Leonardo da Vinci.

In literature: Goethe, Homer, Shakespeare, Cervantes, Montaigne.

You can find for yourself your own examples in art. By focusing on great works of art and the great creators of this art, you can increase the scale and value of your performance.

On the level of the Invisible Clown, or the higher level, you will no longer be concerned by stage fright; on the contrary, at this same level you cannot help but share your knowledge with the public, as well as the other three levels mentioned above — it's when you still want to prove your efficacy to the public.

In chapters 10 – 14 we will examine this higher level in more detail. More than that, my aim is to research and find an answer to the following question: how exactly do we get to that fourth level, how do we get to our Invisible Clown?

LESSON 8. CHARACTER — OUR CENTER OF GRAVITY

In order to achieve a greater degree of relaxation, to feel comfortable, free, and to understand ourselves, let's play a little, goof around, become children again for a little while. We are not going to put on any airs, we are not going to play at being children, we are going to become children. I call this the warm-up. We have to change how we look and how we do things, become a circle, then a triangle, and then a square, then become hard or soft, depending on your figure. And your voice should sound like a bass, falsetto, or soprano. Are you ready?

Set the video camera or smartphone up so that it can take a wide-angle view of your room. Switch on the camera and try to walk around the room for two minutes as a triangle, and then two minutes as a circle. Get a feel for what works best for you. Each time make some noise, such as 'Mi-Ma-Mo' for example, first in a bass voice, then a falsetto, and finally in a soprano voice. Nobody is going to see you, so don't be shy, be as silly as you want.

In everyday life this warm-up will help you in different situations. In your associations with your subordinates you will be slightly square or slightly triangular in your movements and in your decision-making, and when you are winding down with your colleagues, you will be the opposite, more rounded and informal.

You can also think up a dream for your personality, its dream determines its scale. A 'dumb blonde's' dream, or 'a 'Nobel Laureate's' dream, anything goes! Either one of these characters can be unbelievably charismatic, as long as they are true to themselves.

EXERCISE 9 ●▨▨▨▨▨▨▨▨▨▨▨▨▨▨▨▨▨▨

Now the time has come for a real exercise. It will help you to be true to yourself, to be precise and convincing during negotiations, as well as during photo and video shoots, and performances on stage in front of the public.

Let's try and feel our center of gravity, as we discussed above.

Since your smartphone is already set up from your warm-up, we can start. Don't forget to prepare a text, the same one you have used in previous exercises.

You will need to read your text eight times — four times in a static state, and four times in an active state.

Switch on your video camera, and at a distance of approximately two meters from the camera read the text standing on one spot. Each time your center of gravity should move. Be guided by your instincts. Maybe your voice will come from your tailbone. Then talk from your tailbone.

The second time you do this, your voice should come from your kinetic center, you should be able to hold your center of gravity in your legs, talk from your legs, or more precisely, from your calf muscles.

The third time — when your emotions come into play — your voice will come from your solar plexus.

Let's dedicate the fourth time you do this to your intellect: try to speak from your head, or more accurately, from the nape of your neck. When you read your text out loud, try to look at the camera from time to time; the camera is your viewer. Furthermore, you need to look from your specific center of gravity: do not look with your eyes, but from your center of gravity out through your eyes.

The next four times try doing this same exercise whilst on the move. So move, you can jump up and down, walk around in a circle, it's not important. The main thing is to remember your center of gravity and to speak and look from your specific center of gravity. Also, don't forget to listen to your voice, stop your thoughts, or, as you have done in other exercises, separate yourself from your name, sending, in your imagination, your name into the auditorium. Watch your video recording, analyze it, and find the difference between your performance from your intellectual center of gravity and from your kinetic, instinctive and emotional centers, and so on. Don't forget to watch your warm-up.

Start to ask yourself questions, particularly if there was something you didn't like. Do not turn away from something that you don't like. Even if you are tired, have a rest and try to change it.

We are steadily approaching the topic known as 'State.' I, as someone with many years of experience of performing on stage, can tell you that the state of the Invisible Clown is our charisma, something which is beyond any template, it is our true manifestation of success.

From the first part of the book we learned that timing is the skeleton on which everything we do, or any performance we give, hangs.

From the second part we learned that the character which we create, acts like our muscles. We touched on charisma, and we spoke about the four qualitative levels of works of art, and about some acting techniques.

In the third part of the book we will see that state is the soul of whatever we do, and of our performance, and we will also understand how the Invisible Clown is linked to the Divine, to the Great Viewer.

Part Three
STATE

CHAPTER 10

Drawings in The Sky

If timing is the skeleton of our performance, and character its muscles, then the state of the Invisible Clown is the SOUL of our performance. The soul is our link to the Divine.

Yevgeniy Mironov, a wonderful Russian actor:

'Alla Demidova said that we, as actors,
draw on the sky and the winds take it all away.

This catharsis, however, is a moment that can barely be captured,
a moment of cleansing — on stage or on film — it comes at that time
when you are as honest as you can be. You can't do anything
without this contrition. And in order to confess you have to
find the courage, the strength. It is also important to have
something to say — the viewer will feel this so strongly!
Then everything will make sense.'[19]

---

[19] Yevgeniy Mironov – on 'Uncle Vanya,' ecology, bullying, and catharsis. https://instyle.ru/stars/interview/evgeniy-mironov-o-dyadye-vane-ekologii-khuliganstve-i-katarsise/.

Freddie Mercury
British singer and musician (1946 – 1991)

*'I just burn on stage! The feeling I get from contact with
the audience is much stronger than sex. I like this awakened
state, and I always feel like I want more — more, more, more.
I'm just a musical prostitute!'*[20]

I have heard many times from artistes that being on stage is like a narcotic.

Why is it like that?

At the very moment of our performance, we are in very unusual conditions, we are being watched, dozens, hundreds, or maybe even thousands of people are watching us, and when it comes to television or film, maybe millions. This serves to increase the level of concentration in our minds. We find ourselves at the cutting edge. This environment leads us to an unusual state — in our case, to the state of the Invisible Clown.

In everyday life reaching this state is incredibly difficult, but on stage it is easily achievable. Everything makes sense, the performance itself, and the preparation for it.

Even the public are confined in some way. If you tell a joke in daily life, someone will always talk back to you, laugh at you for a short while, then joke themselves, and your story or joke will not be what you thought it was.

Within the specific rules of behaviour in an auditorium, however, the public are focused solely on the performer, and they are not able to comment on what they see. Then their reaction is restricted to applause and laughter, and here other rules come into play.

I first went on stage as a clown at the Kharkov pioneer's and

[20] https://ru.citaty,net/temy/stsena/

children's center during the new-year holidays in 1983, when the 'Smile' Circus led by the King of Fate presented its shows. In the programme I was introduced as a clown. I performed three acts: 'The Juggler,' 'The Unsuccessful Acrobat,' and 'The Doll.'

I was enthused with an internal drive, which I was experiencing at that time. The eyes of the audience, the little boys, girls, and their parents are watching you. And you in your 14 years are, in essence, still a child yourself, and you can do anything you want with your peers and their parents. Nobody is going to clap you on, nobody is going to make it difficult for you, or interrupt you.

In one sense the public are delighted or hypnotized by a show, and they fall completely under a performer's spell. Usually people who are not in the acting profession work between 8 – 12 hours a day. A circus artiste performs on stage on average for between 5 – 20 minutes, exactly as long as their act lasts. Moreover, a circus artiste may feel their output, and their tiredness, to a greater or lesser extent perhaps than people who work in an office all day long.

There is a difference, however; usually after work, people want to go home. I don't know how it is for other artistes, but several times I have wanted to stay on stage after my act or my show has come to an end, despite the fact that I am physically tired.

On stage everything is as clear as it can be: the sound, the lighting, and the public. When you return backstage, however, you are hit with dozens of concerns and problems. What you are going to eat, drink, when you are going to get home, which school to choose for your child, what time the next day's rehearsal is, whether you are going to buy that house or not, whether your back hurts, what you are going to say to your clients, and so on. The cares come back and the state of the Invisible Clown leaves.

When we are on stage we are watched by hundreds or maybe thousands of eyes, but we try to keep our minds under control for the duration of our performance. Thanks to this concentration we experience the state of the Invisible Clown. This is our narcotic.

A MUG AND A DROPLET OF WATER

The lighter a person is, the less the laws act upon them, the easier their attitude to life is, the closer they are to the Divine, as well as to other people.

I filled this bottle this morning from the waters of the Pacific Ocean just outside San Francisco. I pour the water into a mug. I splash some of the water onto the floor. We see thousands of individual droplets on the floor.

Although these droplets are not dependent on one another, this is the same water that was in the cup, and, moreover, that same water, which this morning was in the Pacific Ocean. In other words there is an essence of the entire ocean in each separate droplet.

There is still the mug that this water was poured into, which thinks it is what it is, a mug, and there is such a thing as an ocean. That is to say, the mug thinks that it is the owner. Mugs come in all shapes and sizes, and we can pour this water wherever we want, even into an ashtray, or we can make fresh water from this water, and then make soup or a coffee from it. Water is neutral, there is humility in water, it does not resist and yet there is an enormous strength within it.

All mugs have boundaries, but water does not have boundaries. All mugs break sooner or later no matter what, because they are fragile. And water cannot put up any resistance at all. It is transferred from vessel to vessel, from state to state, and it can become ice, or steam.

If we imagine that water, or a droplet, represents a person's soul, and the mug represents their body, then inside each of us there is a drop, the essence of which is an enormous ocean. The ocean is so deep it is bottomless, and its shorelines are our illusions.

When I look at the public in the auditorium, it is through this same metaphor that I see 2,750 droplets from one and the same ocean. Forgive me, 2,751 droplets from one and the same ocean: I forgot about myself.

Our names and surnames are the edges of our mug, which separate us from the great ocean. Imagine, if you will, that there are currently around 7 billion people living on Earth, that's 7 billion mugs, inside each of which are 7 billion droplets from the great ocean.

In life, as on stage, people will follow you if you can reach that same little droplet. When we socialize with other people, and we see this huge drop of water inside them, this enormous potential for developing themselves, we are interacting with that great ocean. If we socialize with people in this way, we cannot do anyone any harm at all.

In everyday life, unfortunately, we almost always find ourselves socializing with mugs. Mugs socialize with mugs, unconsciously singling out who is the cooler, the richer, the more beautiful and more successful among them, and as a result these mugs, or our weaknesses, do not bring people together, on the contrary, they divide them.

Mugs are our force of resistance, because the mug wants to be the boss of this great ocean. It thinks that it is immortal. It thinks that it is the Divine.

A mug gives a lot of advice and it imposes limits, as though it knows what is right. Water really does know. Water is what it is, and takes on any form that it is offered.

'*Everything you see,*
Has a single visibility,
Just a shape,
But the essence nobody can see...'[21]

That droplet from the great ocean is the UNIFYING factor in our souls. It is a droplet, and there is our Invisible Clown.

Not only does a droplet unite us into a single whole, it connects us to that enormous ocean, in other words, with the Divine, the Great Viewer.

THE JOURNEY OF THE TRIANGLES.
THE INVISIBLE CLOWN AND HIS LINK
TO THE GREAT VIEWER

In order to understand the idea of the triangles, which is an idea that makes the journey to the Invisible Clown easier, we should understand that in any phenomenon, in anything we are planning to do, we have to find and observe three forces. Let's name these three forces an active force, a resisting force, and a neutralizing force.

Let's say I have a passion, a strong desire to build a house. Unfortunately, however, I have a problem, a huge resisting force, I don't have sufficient resources. I want to borrow money from my friends and raise funds, or maybe I am planning to take out a bank loan, or I will try and sell something, but nothing works out, I am running out of options.

My desire, my passion to build a house is an active force, and my budget is a passive, or a resisting force.

In general people call the resisting force Murphy's Law, and we don't usually take this force fully into account, for example,

---

[21] Khayyam O. Rubaiyat, – M.:Eksmo, 2019

when we are late for an important meeting because we were in a traffic jam.

What then, in terms of building a house, could be a neutralizing, or a third, force?

Suddenly, when you are not really thinking about anything, you conclude a lucrative contract or you are the beneficiary of an inheritance, or something similar.

In other words, this third force could be called the force of providence. Some time later you find that a chance sequence of events did not happen by chance at all, and without the help of the Divine you would not have built your house.

Or another very simple example, your children ordered pancakes for breakfast. You don't want to get up earlier than usual, but your love for your children forces you out of bed.

Your children's order for pancakes is an active force, and your desire for sleep is a resisting force, but your love for your children is a third force. There you are standing in the kitchen already, in your left hand you are holding a cup of morning coffee, and in your right hand you are pouring a portion of pancake mix into a hot saucepan.

The three forces can be observed clearly in politics. Power is an active force, opposition is a resisting force, and the third force might be a 'black swan,' an event, which is impossible to predict but which nevertheless changes the course of history on a fundamental level.

In itself a 'black swan' is completely neutral, it sides with neither one nor the other. The active force and the resisting force are constantly swapping places.

Now on the basis of these three forces let's examine the triad: Mikhail Usov — the Clown — the Invisible Clown.

This will send you on a journey to the Great Viewer.

Mikhail Usov is a resisting force, a minus.

The clown is the child within us, the active force, a plus.

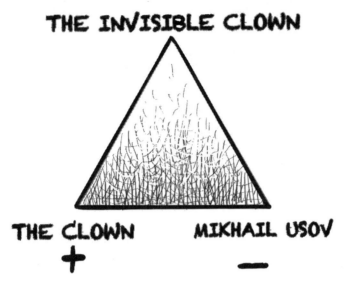

This illustrates a triangle; at the base are: Clown + Mikhail Usov − and the Invisible Clown is at the top.

The Invisible Clown is a balance, a state, in which there is no comprehension of the good or the bad, and there is no duality. It is a neutralizing force.

The Clown grows because of Mikhail Usov. In this sequence, when Mikhail Usov is passive and the Clown is active, this is when the Invisible Clown manifests itself and we experience that wonderful state.

When the triad is arranged in the correct order, it is a pathway that promises an encounter with the Great Viewer.

This encounter emerges in the form of the Great Viewer's triad. This looks like fantasy, because discerning this encounter using the mind alone is impossible, unless we can touch upon this with the help of the creative imagination of the Clown.

For myself I have defined this as follows: since the phenomenon of the Invisible Clown rests on three pillars

— Mikhail Usov, the Clown, and the Invisible Clown — it is possible that the phenomenon of the Great Viewer also rests on three forces. I have named these forces as follows:

The Great Viewer
a passive force, a minus
The Doer-Non-Doer
an active force, a plus
The Invisible Viewer
a neutral force

Imagine if you will that the Great Viewer is very keen to see the Invisible Clown's show. As a result of the Great Viewer's powerful active desire, they have to keep this under control and it becomes a passive force. In view of this the active force of the Doer-Non-Doer grows.

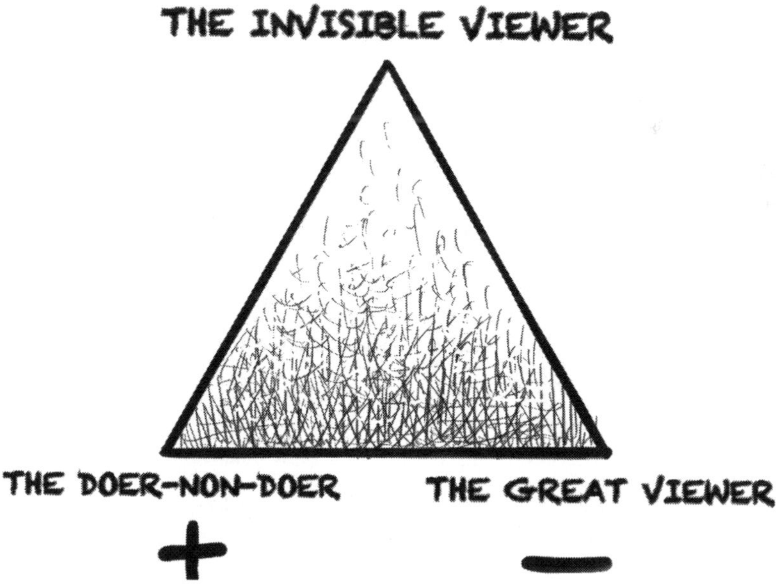

This illustration shows a triangle. At the base are: The DOER-NON-DOER + THE GREAT VIEWER — and the INVISIBLE VIEWER is at the top

The Doer-Non-Doer is the person who, in doing nothing, actually does EVERYTHING. This again sounds absurd. Look at nature: it just exists. Look at the Universe, which, as scientists confirm, came into being thanks to the big bang: it also just exists.

The Invisible Viewer is a neutral force, which balances the minus of the Great Viewer, its strong desire, and the plus of the Doer-Non-Doer.

A confluence of the three forces of the Invisible Clown and the three forces of the Great Viewer represent our connection with the Divine that we have been seeking for so long in this book. Or, in other words, the Great Viewer watches the Invisible Clown's show.

Let's go back to Rembrandt and his painting 'The Return of the Prodigal Son.' Now the sense of this painting is clear.

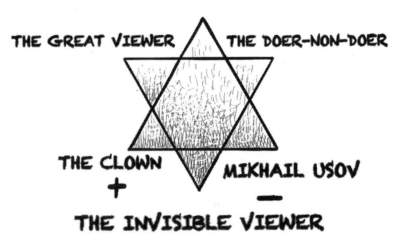

This illustration represents the Star of David. At the base are: THE CLOWN + THE INVISIBLE VIEWER, and MIKHAIL USOV — on the top are THE GREAT VIEWER — THE INVISIBLE CLOWN, and the DOER-NON-DOER +

As in the Star of David that you can see in the illustration above, the work of Rembrandt is dedicated to an encounter with the Divine.

The hands of the father illustrate the triangle pointing downwards, and the head of the son and his shoulders represent a triangle that is moving upwards. They intersect at the heart. They intersect in love.

We can feel that unity without being in the state of the Invisible Clown. Therefore, we love our children just like that, without any conditions of any kind. This is what unconditional love is.

LESSON 9

We will dedicate the last three lessons to the state of the Invisible Clown. In the previous lessons we worked on timing and character, eradicating templates. Timing and character are our performance techniques. The state of the Invisible Clown relates to our consciousness.

Immersion in the state of the Invisible Clown is almost always an intentional action. It is a process, which is fostered by beauty — a perfectly selected location for your action, the light, colour, design, style and so on. It is especially important to build this atmosphere when performing in public.

In order to be a charismatic person you have to experience the state of the Invisible Clown. To experience this state, you have to delve into the present moment and settle there — this is how you can help your partners and viewers to also be in the present moment, and that means to experience this state. A carefully arranged atmosphere helps you to be in the present moment.

The great German author Goethe, when he entertained guests in his home in Weimar, would change the atmosphere, so that it corresponded to his guests' tastes. He would even order the walls to be painted a different colour, the interiors to be changed, and different pictures to be hung on the walls, and a new menu to be drawn up.[22]

For me, this is a wonderful example of how we can be more creative, more conscious in how we approach life. We can be more active, changing the atmosphere for our friends and business partners, or just changing it to suit ourselves.

EXERCISE 10 ●▨▨▨▨▨▨▨▨▨▨▨▨▨▨▨▨▨▨▨▨

You will need to arrange a small set of some kind in the room that you are in. Fantasize a little and create your own interior design, your own atmosphere that reflects the positive. You could arrange your small set around your bookshelf, or a fireplace with a burning fire in it; or put small trees in a pot to the left or right of you, put a rug on the floor, or possibly put up a writing desk. Don't forget about the pictures on the walls. You will also need your wardrobe, which we have already used in previous lessons, a video camera or smartphone, and of course, your wonderful text.

Set the video camera or smartphone in a way that allows you to see the whole ensemble you have created. Don't be in such a hurry to start to read your text.

Take three or four steps back from the set you have created. Look at it from a short distance away for around two minutes. Stop all your thoughts completely. Then imagine yourself standing in this space and reading your text. Have you imagined yourself doing that?

Then go back to your original position, back to your set.

---

[22] Eckermann I.P... Conversations with Goethe. – M.: RIPOL classic, 2020.

Feel like you are an indivisible part of the atmosphere that you have created. As though a picture, or the fireplace, or a tree, regardless of whether they are behind or to the side of you, is a part of your body, like your hand or your foot.

Feel like your whole set is alive, as though it has a tongue and eyes and that it can speak and see. If you do everything slowly, stopping your thoughts, you will definitely be enveloped by the state of the Invisible Clown.

Now read your extract in what is a new atmosphere for you, and in this wonderful state. When you read your text, be conscious of yourself, listen to your voice to help achieve this. Record yourself on video. Watch the video recording, analyze your performance. There should be harmony in everything from the set to the way you read your text out loud.

Maybe your voice should be quieter, or the opposite, it should be louder, and your performance should be a little slower or more focused. Remember that all movements need to be made separately and consciously.

Don't forget to mentally stick your thoughts on the back of the chair or on your name, separating yourself from yourself. If you really do experience the state of the Invisible Clown, there is no need to worry about the above, just let it be.

In the next exercise I will send you on a real trip. You will need to spend a little money. Prepare a small suitcase with enough clothes for three days.

CHAPTER 11

The King of Hearts

This chapter is about my third teacher, the King of Hearts. It is about how he taught me common sense, how he revealed the meaning of life, and gave me direction.

THE PERSPECTIVE

My searches led me to a revelation: in order to be a funny and convincing clown, I had to experience a mystical state of consciousness. I looked for this wonderful state everywhere. After reading the book *In Search of the Miraculous* by Pyotr Ouspensky, I understood where I had to search for it. This book underlines especially that a human being can forget who they are. If they forget who they are, they become a machine. And a machine works on the principle of stimulus-response. Only when they experience a moment for real do they stop being a machine. Let's try to be conscious of ourselves right now.

In this very moment, reading this sentence, we remember who we are, but as soon as some other suggestion comes in we forget ourselves, because a chain of associations is set in motion that takes us away from who we are.

I was a passionate vegetarian for nine years and I slimmed down. I didn't eat anything that had eyes. My favourite chicken, steaks, turkey, and even fish, as fish have eyes too, ran, flew, and swam out of my life. Some people felt sorry for me, while others would joke with me about it.

I intentionally shifted the emphasis towards vegetarianism, and this topic really did take me away from the PRESENT moment. Now, however, whenever I pay attention to now, we again return to THIS moment happening right now. Is that the case for you? Did you come back to this moment?

There is no future and no past in the present moment. Normally, people 'wander away' from it, following their thoughts. When you read about the present moment you are there, but if the conversation drifts onto another subject, for instance about vegetarianism, and correspondingly, a new set of associative connections arises, it's as if you fall away from the present. Naturally, you are still there bodily, but your consciousness is closed off, as if by a veil, or by thoughts, associations and so on.

This truth shocked me so deeply that I devoured a great number of books that dealt with the present moment. In the majority of cases these books described how important it is to be in the present moment and how to find your way there. What I did not find anywhere, however, was how to remain in this moment and how not to depart from it.

Some books discussed meditation, others prayer. I could remember sitting in the lotus position and looking every now and again at a bare wall, and sometimes into the midst of a candle flame. I chased away my thoughts. I also remembered how on the streets of Moscow I would repeat the same prayer again and again: 'Lord, forgive me for I have sinned, Lord, forgive me for I have sinned.'

Ouspensky writes that we cannot master the present moment ourselves, and we need a teacher to show us how to do this.

A teacher…where in the enormous city of Moscow could I find a real teacher? It seemed like all the teachers lived in India or in the Middle East.

My friend the famous Cream Clown told me that there was a school of the Fourth Way in Moscow. Ouspensky also wrote about the school of the Fourth Way.

The first way is that of the fakir, who sacrifices his physical body in exchange for an understanding of the world.

The second way is that of the monk, and a monk keeps his own passions in check.

The third way is that of the yogi, who disciplines his mind.

The fourth way combines and interprets the first three. This is a wonderful journey, one of maximum consciousness, a path of freedom from the power of our illusions, and from templates, from automatism.

This method is personal to me. I liked the Fourth Way, because nobody needs to know what you are doing. Life as it is provides an individual with an abundance of opportunities for development.

You don't have to sit on broken glass, or pray, or meditate in the lotus position. On the contrary, you should do whatever it is you usually do — speak to people, perform on stage, be a father, drill a hole with a drill and so on — but do it consciously. Be so natural and so yourself that nobody can really find out or understand what it is you are actually doing.

The reader might say: 'How does this work? Can you give an example? So there I am drilling a hole with a drill, it is clear to anyone what I am doing, I am drilling a hole.'

The Fourth Way proposes doing what you are doing consciously. After all, at that moment when I am drilling the hole, my mind may be wandering off in any direction: it may end up in Paris, or in the French embassy, or at a meeting that's already in the past; my mind might procrastinate over someone's point of view on something, or I in my mind I might be defending my own point of view and so on.

If you just drill a hole, stopping your thoughts, then, as a rule, your hole will be better and you might possibly experience the state of the Invisible Clown.

We are only talking here of internal processes that accompany our activities. Naturally, everyone can see that we are drilling a hole, and this is the external side of what we are doing, but what we are really doing is stopping our thoughts. Moreover, we need to stop our thoughts in such a way that nobody understands that we are stopping our thoughts.

If somebody understands that at a given moment we are stopping our thoughts, it means we are imitating this process and we are not fully conscious of ourselves.

The Fourth Way differs in that it is not a permanent path. It doesn't have any specific shape, or institutions, and it comes on, develops, and leaves according to its own laws.

When its 'work' is done, that is to say when the objective we have set has been achieved, the Fourth Way disappears from that place, it disappears in its given form, and possibly continues in another form somewhere else.

The Cream Clown told me that a true teacher of the Fourth Way lives in California, a follower of Gurdjieff and Ouspensky. Although in the real world he is a wine grower and an antiques collector.

In order to get into the school of the Fourth Way in Moscow I had to listen to a few introductory lectures.

The first lecture was about the fact that the focus of our attention always depends on external events. Let's say if someone shouts 'Idiot!' harshly and loudly, all your attention will be focused on that exclamation: somebody is experiencing fear, worry, someone else begins to talk about the person who shouted out, and somebody else wants to get out of that place quickly. In this case we identify with that exclamation, and we almost become that exclamation ourselves.

At another introductory lecture they discussed what a 'person cannot do.' Someone finishes school or university, they find work, they have a family, they innovate, they work, they bring up, they marry, they divorce, and they die and so on. This is all in accordance with a programme, with a template, and in this case everything HAPPENS to that person.

When someone is conscious they can see these programmes, these templates, and they find they have a CHOICE: to act according to the template or not. Then they have an opportunity to not be a part of that programme, but to DO something for themselves. A person like that more often than not does the same things: they graduate from college or from university, and they find work, they innovate, they work, they marry, they have a family, they bring up children, they divorce, and they die and so on, but they do it CONSCIOUSLY. What is more, they have a connection to a higher power.

There is a theory that says that a conscious person is able to survive their own death. A biological body, naturally, dies and a specific life programme has been built into that body. There is, however, something else in us (Ouspensky called this the 'astral body'), which is capable of surviving death.

I have heard many times, and I can confirm this myself, that an elderly person never feels their age, even if their body is growing older and is ailing. I began to be conscious of myself for the first time at around three years of age and my earliest memories are from that time. This sense of myself is exactly the same now, when I am 53 years of age. This feeling has not aged along with my biological body. The same can be said of old men. A consciousness of yourself, of what makes you who you are, is always the same and is independent of age.

It cannot be ruled out that this same consciousness of who you are, can actually survive your biological body. If you are conscious of yourself, you can, at the point of death, if it is not very sudden (for example, you are not run over by a tram like Berlioz from 'The Master and Margarita'), try to explore this point of transition. Remember the death of Socrates as described by Plato in the 'Phaedo' dialogue. Socrates went consciously, even though it was a punishment.

If you live according to a template, however, if you live unconsciously, you do not have a choice at all. The thought of exploring this process will never enter your head because you will come under the influence of very different emotions — ranging possibly from shock, to panic, to self-pity.

I say again, this is just a theory, and we can try and test it when our time comes, — or we can do things according to a template, and just die as we are programmed to. In order to conduct this experiment we have to prepare for it, because none of us knows the date of our death. We prepare for this with the help of our consciousness, by being conscious of ourselves in any situation, whatever life might give us.

I remember my first impression of the introductory lectures. Since by that time I had already graduated from the clowning studio where we were taught acting techniques, I was well acquainted with exercises around attention. I was, however, shocked by the fact that at the school of the Fourth Way there was a connection with a higher power, given all the other similar techniques. I sensed its presence from the very first lecture.

It was a warm early evening. I was reading what is still my favourite book right up to now 'The Ingenious Don Quixote of La Mancha' by Miguel de Cervantes. At some point a small fly landed on my left hand. So as to flatten it or at least push it away, I raised my right hand, but then I held back because I clearly heard a thought: 'Stop.... Look at the fly.'

I looked at the fly and I could see the reflection of a rainbow in its wings. Its huge eyes, four small, transparent winglets. I could see how perfect this creature was, so I could not kill this insect.

The fly crawled around my arm for a moment and then flew away.

This small event, which was completely trivial and banal, had overflowed into an experience of eternity. Why had this happened?

The reason is because when I was examining the fly for the first time I had been conscious that I was led by a higher power within myself. I was aware of my own existence. It was so natural and so wonderful that it seemed to me that this was our true, simple, human state, of which we are, for some reason, bereft.

After that I was no longer in any doubt that we do have a link to a higher power and that this higher power lives in us and can tell us 'Stop!' — and what is more it can show us, or advise us what to do.

THE FIRST MEETING

Five years had passed since I had begun to study at the school of the Fourth Way. Somehow I ended up on a tour in the capital of France. There was a center of the school of the Fourth Way in Paris as well, and several students were studying there.

When I had some days to myself I would sit in on their lectures. Once we were told that a teacher of the Fourth Way, who was a wine grower from California, whom I would later know as the King of Hearts, was planning to visit Paris in two weeks time. A female student, Dama Drama, said it would help me if I met him personally.

Two days later Dama Drama told me that the teacher was inviting me to dinner at a Paris restaurant, and that I could ask him whatever I wanted.

All this time I had been excited to meet this individual who was constantly in that state of consciousness that I had been seeking for so long. The day before this event I went to the Notre-Dame Cathedral in Paris.

I didn't actually go into the cathedral: there were a great many tourists. I went down to the embankment of the River Seine. It was a wonderful evening and I understood that the following day at about that time I would see the true Teacher. I began to think over the sequence of questions and how I could formulate them accurately.

The calm flow of the Seine, the reflection of the autumnal trees in its waters, the bridges, and the cathedral itself, the scent of roasting chestnuts, awoke in me the state of the Invisible Clown.

In my mind I began to ask the King of Hearts questions, and the answers to these questions suddenly came from the Invisible Clown. They were so convincing that there was no longer any sense in asking the King of Hearts these questions. I received five answers to my five questions. By the time I met the King of Hearts I no longer had a single question left. It was as though I had been liberated, I felt empty inside.

The next day at the appointed time I went to the restaurant not far from Rue Froissart. I remembered my experience of getting into the clowning studio, and I wore a suit as I had back then.

Suddenly I felt like someone was looking at the nape of my neck. I turned around and saw a tall man, who was smiling at me generously. A huge golden crown was glowing behind the King of Hearts's head — it was the setting sun. There was a group of some fifteen people around the Teacher. They were wearing whatever they wanted. Next to them were suitcases with Delta luggage tags. They had only just flown in from San Francisco. They were all silent. We went into the restaurant.

The waiters fussed over the luggage for a while. The King of Hearts showed everyone where to sit. He sat Dama Drama and I next to each other. We were given a menu and everyone remained silent as they had before. The King of Hearts advised me to order the round clams in a white wine sauce.

We ordered our chosen dishes. Through his interpreter the King of Hearts said that I could ask him my questions now. I explained how I had prepared for our meeting and had found answers to all my questions.

The King of Hearts was silent for a long time, and then said:

'When we are in the state of the present moment, we don't have any questions.'

They handed us the bread with olive oil and basil, but suddenly I understood that I did want to ask a question nevertheless, which had only come to my mind right at the last second.

I said:

'I do have a question...'

Everyone stopped chewing and looked at the King of Hearts. He also put down his piece of bread. He looked at me again for a long time and then nodded to his interpreter, so they could interpret my question.

I asked:

'Does vegetarianism affect the state of consciousness?'

The King of Hearts, after taking a small sip of wine and patting his lips dry with a white linen napkin, said in a soft voice:

'God created the chicken for eating, and swans for beauty…'

We again turned to the table. Everyone was silent. The King of Hearts continued, not just for me any more but for everyone else.

The interpreter interpreted what he was saying:

'You can eat whatever you want. Just don't eat too much. What is important is not what you eat, but how you eat it.'

This meal, after a nine-year abstinence from meat, put an end to my vegetarianism. I tried a delicious steak with a black pepper sauce.

The words 'what's important is how you eat,' soon turned into an exercise that was proposed by the King of Hearts, so we remained silent while we were eating. The idea of this was for us to taste the food, which was designed to help us be more conscious as we were consuming our food. Thanks to this exercise I began to see myself, and others, in a better light.

The King of Hearts said it was good that we could only do one thing. If we were to chew and speak at the same time, it would be hard for us to warm to the taste of the food. Apart from that, in eating our food we would not be able to hear the sound of our voices when we spoke, and as a result we would not know what we were talking about.

We would turn into a talking and chewing head, and we would think and talk in templates. I learned that the King of Hearts had not eaten alone for thirty years. He was always traveling or with a group of around twelve to fifteen people. This crowd would sometimes fluctuate.

DAMA DRAMA

The following day we met again at an antiques auction. The King of Hearts, dressed in a bright orange sports jacket and a snow-white cloth cap, wandered slowly around the huge auction halls. He was holding Dama Drama's hand. Dama Drama was wearing an elegant straw hat, which the King of Hearts had given her. His entire entourage walked behind him.

Dama Drama worked as his secretary. She kept track of Parisian cultural life. I later befriended her. Dama was German and she had come to Paris when she was a little girl with her parents during the Second World War. She lived outside Paris with her husband in an enormous mansion.

Her husband was a popular dramatist in Paris. The most famous theatres staged his plays. Dama Drama entertained many famous guests in her house, representatives of the Parisian beau-monde. Dama Drama organized literary meetings, and I was even lucky enough to perform with my clowning acts in her large drawing room

What struck me about Dama Drama, however, was something else. She once showed me Paris in her old Mercedes. Dama Drama could speak German, French, and English. She spoke English to me. She knew that I had almost no English, but in spite of this she took me on an excursion around Paris, showing me the houses where great French writers, poets, and kings lived. Dama Drama did not park the car because parking is a big problem in Paris. She would stop her car right in the middle of small side streets, blocking any movement either side. After this she would tell me the history of one house or another for a sufficiently long time. I only understood two words from my 'guide's' explanations: 'Victor Hugo,' as she would always repeat his name.

Behind us a real dramatic street show called 'The traffic queue' was unfolding. The cars were beeping their horns so loudly and in unison that I could hardly hear Dama Drama's trained actor's voice. She though was unruffled by this. She would jab her long index finger at the cars blowing their horns and say: 'Negative emotions...' (At the school of the Fourth Way there had been an exercise on the first day about not expressing negative emotions).

THE MEAL OPPOSITE SAINT-GERMAN-DES-PRÉS

After the antique auction we all went to lunch at the famous café Les Deux Magots opposite the cathedral of Saint-Germain-des-Pres. Since the XIX Century this café has enjoyed popularity among the literary and cultural elite of the capital. Simone de Beauvoir, Jean-Paul-Sartre, and Albert Camus have all visited here.

We sat on the street at round tables, which were arranged at the request of the King of Hearts. He asked that the chairs be moved into one row so that we could see the cathedral and what was happening around us. As he had at the meal the night before, the King of Hearts said where everyone was going to sit, and he sat himself in the middle.

As he pointed to the passers-by and to the cars on the street, the King of Hearts said that it is useful to observe life, just as you would a play in a theatre.

As was customary, everyone was silent.

The King of Hearts did not talk much. He didn't really say much at all at any time.

Suddenly, a man approached the café from the cathedral side and it was evident he was not feeling quite himself. He was heading straight for the next table where an elderly couple were sitting, and began to pester the grey-haired man loudly. Dama Drama said that this grey-haired man was a famous French politician.

This strange man did not calm down.

The King of Hearts said: 'Pay attention to the people in the café. They are all involved in this charade,' and sure enough when I looked at the visitors in the café, I could see that they were all looking at this crazy man.

The politician's wife began to defend him. Like a true 'bodyguard' she jumped up from her seat and began to shout.

After some time the strange man calmed down and left.

The King of Hearts said: 'This was a good example of feminine dominance. He did not defend himself, she defended him.' This was how I learned about 'feminine dominance.' It is also known as motherly dominance. A mother defends and brings up her children, explaining to them what is right and what is wrong. To Native Americans, for example, a mother represents the earth, as my friend the vocalist Sandakva from the Wendake tribe explained to me.

A mother protects her children. Try to get up close to a female bear when she is nurturing her cubs, she will see you as a threat. In other words, a mother wants everything to go according to the programme. Anything that is not part of the programme she sees as a danger and begins to go on the defensive, protecting the programme. Therefore, the protective mother lives in all of us, irrespective of whether you are a man or a woman.

The rules of our behaviour in society are also programmed. We don't even give this any thought and we are not interested in who wrote this programme — we just fulfill it.

Our concern about how other people see us is also a programme. More often than not our actions are motivated by a desire for people to see us in a good light. Let's say an elderly man gets into a tram and we give up our seat for him not because he is an elderly man and it is difficult for him to stand up, but more likely out of concern that the other passengers might think bad of us if we are young and we continued to sit down.

When we see an elderly man getting on and the impulse to give up our seat appears out of empathy, at that moment we are more conscious because we are SERVING. I have given the simplest example. How many complex examples are there though? Let's say we are often unable to say what we really think about a person, or about some sort of phenomenon out loud, because we are afraid that we might encounter judgment from those around us. In actual fact it is the mothering programme in us that says: 'Don't get involved,' or 'Do you need to more than anyone else?'

This thought: 'What do people think of me?' is one of the aspects of feminine dominance and it is this dominance that represents these same behavioural templates.

In our case, when the woman defended the politician, she defended him the way a mother would her children.

THE CHOCOLATE SWEET

For these few days the King of Hearts kept me in his entourage. Sometimes it seemed to me that he was Woland himself from 'The Master and Margarita' with his entourage on the streets of Paris.

We would always have lunch, evening meals and breakfast together, and we would always maintain the same etiquette: the King of Hearts would personally show each one of his 'courtiers' where to sit.

In this period of time we attended antique auctions on several occasions in the Louvre.

It was hard to get the King of Hearts's attention and very easy to lose it. When he spoke to you, it seemed that he was talking to you as a friend, as if you had know him for 100 years. In actual fact, he was like that to everyone.

The following day we walked around the Louvre. The King of Hearts was interested in French paintings and Louis XIV furniture, the 'Sun King.'

After the Louvre, the King of Hearts and two other people went into an antique shop, and the rest, including myself, stopped and waited for our teacher opposite a bakery shop. The window was showing off marzipan cakes shaped like piglets. On each of the piglets a name of some kind was spelled out in dark chocolate. Suddenly, one of us burst out laughing and went into the shop and bought a piglet with the name Brian. It turned out in the meantime that the name of a very wonderful and excellent artist in the group was Brian.

Everyone began to break bits off the marzipan sweet. I could see the sorrowful eyes of the real Brian, who was standing next to me; they were like the eyes of this piglet and it just seemed so funny to me that I began to laugh out loud at the artist. Unexpectedly, I saw a hand holding the marzipan sweet in front of my nose.

I thought that I was being given a piece of Brian. The hand, however, shoved the marzipan sweet in my face and smeared the piglet over my cheeks and nose. This, of course, was the hand of the King of Hearts. He had appeared decisively from out of the blue like Zeus the thunder-bearer; he hit me with the marzipan sweet as quick as lightning. I felt like a clown at the circus who had a pie slapped in his face.

'A joke that harms another person is not a joke,' said the King of Hearts.

His secretary went into the shop and purchased an enormous box of confectioneries. The King of Hearts undid the enormous white bow himself, opened the metal box and, walking around everyone in turn, he put a sweet in everyone's mouth himself.

This was a surprising spectacle: fifteen people stood in a circle and the King of Hearts was putting a sweet in their mouths one by one.

If I am honest, I don't like sweet things that much, but it was hard to refuse. All this was from that same feminine dominance of course. The King of Hearts was on his third trip round the circle when he approached me to put the next sweet in my mouth, and I was still chewing the second sweet. I said, with my mouth full, that I couldn't eat anything else. He called his interpreter over and asked them to interpret for me: 'it's an exercise for us: when we are eating, we don't talk.'

THE FATHER

The time I spent with the King of Hearts was coming to an end, because I had to leave a short time later for Belgium on the tour. We met again, however, a month later in Paris.

In the space of that month a great deal had changed for me.

My father had died. He passed away from cancer in a hospital in Germany.

While we were working in Belgium, my brother had called me and said that our father had been admitted to hospital and he did not have long to live. On the first day off, I hired a car and drove to see my father for two days. My father had lost some weight, and he said that we should not worry because he was taking tablets, which made him feel significantly better.

My father was administered morphine. His illness was at a stage already where nothing more could be done. My father knew about this but did not tell anyone. In Germany doctors are obliged by law to inform their patients about the diagnosis and how long they have to live. If their patient does not understand German, they are assigned an interpreter.

We spent these two days together.

That night I returned to Bruges in Belgium directly from the hospital. My father had walked with me to the car park, and the road passed through a small wooded park. About half way along this route, in the oak wood, he stopped and said that he wanted to go back to the ward because it was difficult for him to walk.

We hugged. There was a deathly silence and not the slightest breath of wind. Only very occasionally would overripe acorns disturb the silence, falling here and there from the trees like large drops of rain. I understood that this would be the last time I would see and hug my father. This was how it turned out.

A week later we were performing a show at one of the most beautiful theatres in Antwerp, the Koningin Elisabethzaal. I was already wearing my make-up ten minutes before the start of the show. My brother called me on my mobile. He said that our father had passed away.

We always started that show with a scene around the piano. I just stood there and looked statically into the auditorium. On that occasion I did still look statically at the public but tears were running down my cheeks, it was impossible to stop them. No matter how many times I would say to myself: 'Mikhail Usov go into the auditorium' — nothing helped. It was not Mikhail Usov who was crying, it was the clown. I barely got through the show. I don't remember what the reaction of the public was, and this was completely unimportant for me.

The following day, I returned to Germany to bury my father. It was a wonderful sunny day, Mum and I walked behind the coffin. Several times in the course of the funeral ceremony I experienced the state of the Invisible Clown. I understood that death is as much of a secret as birth. There are, really, only two fundamental events in a person's life: their birth and their death.

COMMON SENSE

After the death of my father I could sense that my father was now the King of Hearts.

My meeting with the King had made such a deep impression on me that I did a lot of strange things trying to follow his teachings and be conscious, to be in the present moment. In each Belgian theatre where we did our show, I would forget my enormous long clown boots and my hat. A clown's boots are the most important part of their costume. My dear clowning partners would laugh at me, and the French impresario monsieur Julienne, when he noticed that I was reading Gurdzhiev's book, said to me: 'Please, stop reading that book — it's dangerous and you are like a son to me.'

The theatres sent my boots and hat by post on to the next theatres where we were due to perform. Fortunately the postal service works well in Belgium, otherwise where would I find a pair of clown's boots and a yellow hat in this small country?

A large house had been rented for us in Belgium, which was full of antiques. The owner of the mansion, a doctor of medicine, Monsieur Bob, was a good guy and he allocated me a room with XVIII Century furniture. I lived like I was in the Louvre. Having immersed myself in the atmosphere of that time, I began to use candles instead of electric light. I put one of them on an elegant desk, and nowadays we would call it a writing desk. I continued reading Gurdzhiev's book — a dangerous one in monsieur Julienne's opinion. He had not been wrong, because without noticing the smoke, I had burnt this antique XVIII writing desk through with my candle. A fifteen-centimeter hole had formed. There was no smell of burning, on the contrary, there was a fragrance in the air, and it seemed to me that this was linked to the state of the Invisible Clown that I had experienced whilst reading the book.

I thought that I would be fired for sure. Monsieur Bob though looked at the desk with his kind and compassionate eyes, and he then looked at me: 'Don't worry, the desk is insured, just pay for the monthly insurance.' The insurance cost around 72 Euros.

When I returned to Paris a month later and told the King of Hearts about me forgetting my clown's boots and my hat, and burning a hole in the antique desk, he was surprised and said:

'Common sense is needed in everything.'
Some time later he announced to all his students:
'We are all in the same business. We are all clowns.'

The King of Hearts was an unusual traveler. Nobody ever knew where he was going. If it was raining in Paris he would open a newspaper and check if it was sunny in Normandy, and then an hour later he and his entire entourage would be hurrying to Rouen in rented cars. He though may not make it to Rouen, because if he noticed a sign of some sort in himself, he could turn the cars around half way and hurry back to Paris, or to Venice, or to Rome and so on. Therefore, on leaving Paris nobody knew where we would end up by the end of the day, and where we would spend the night. Even the King of Hearts himself didn't know this. If anyone tried to argue with him, and say that we didn't need to go to Venice and should carry on towards Rouen, the King of Hearts would say: 'This is what the higher powers want.'

He listened unquestioningly to the higher powers. Once he

told us: 'If I had three wishes, like in a fairy tale, these three wishes would be: 'Thy will be done,' 'Thy will be done,' and 'Thy will be done.''

The King of Hearts had an indefatigable will. With his height, build, and character he was reminiscent of the Olympic God Zeus. He was someone who admired Italy, and he was a researcher and collector of ancient artifacts. He was reminiscent of the great Goethe, whom Eckermann so wonderfully described in his book 'Conversations with Goethe.' The way he socialized with his students, his love of art and beauty, evoked memories of associations with Leonardo da Vinci from the historiographical novel by Dmitriy Merezhkovskiy, 'The Romance of Leonardo da Vinci.'

For all his internal and external strength the King of Hearts had moments where he seemed completely helpless, like a four-year-old child.

On one occasion I was a witness to him taking his secretaries to task; after he had said what he thought of them, the King of Hearts turned sharply and, feverish and annoyed, he quickly stormed off. He walked maybe fifty meters, stopped for a few seconds, again turned round, and, slowing his stride, he came back a completely different person. Only two minutes had passed from the moment he had walked away to the moment he had returned. He, however, came back as the positive, touching and loving King of Hearts, the way he always was. For me this was a shock, it seemed that he had swallowed his negativity in those two minutes. You won't see that sort of magic in any film.

On one occasion I was lucky enough to complete a cruise with the King of Hearts down the Nile in Egypt. We studied the pyramids, the sphinx, and the ancient temples. Each evening the King of Hearts would go out on deck to watch the sunset.

Later I learned that there is a special note in his schedule: 'To watch the sunset each evening, wherever I can and wherever it's a beautiful sight.'

I know that he often watches the sunset when he travels along the California Pacific coast or around Italy.

To be alongside the King of Hearts is to always be in clover, so it is hard to leave him. I understood then, and I understand now, that our consciousness is an experiment for all of us.

'We come into this world alone
and we also die alone.'[23]

I understood: that in order to be conscious I had to transform my sufferings into consciousness myself. This is what Eckermann wrote about in his book 'Conversations with Goethe:'

'An oak that grew shaded cosily from the wind and the weather
is not a worthy tree — only a century of battling the elements
makes it strong and powerful, so that, having developed fully, it
inspires rapture and wonder in us.'[24]

My teacher brought me to that point where all religions coincide. My teacher infected me with a virus of self-remembering.

The King of Hearts taught me not to take things that we see with our own eyes so seriously. He taught me to be in a place that is beyond words, to see the inexplicable. He taught me to love. He taught me to 'divide and rule' — to have command over yourself, separating yourself from yourself.

---

[23] The Dalai Lama on his Facebook page, 30 April 2013.

[24] Eckermann I.P. Conversations with Goethe. – M.: RIPOL classic, 2020.

CHAPTER 12

Scale and Relativity

This chapter is about how the Invisible Clown, by not controlling anything, supports everything.

BRING YOUR CREATION TO LIFE

The Invisible Clown lives in the moment, in the here and now. He sees what is needed for this to happen and also what would get in his way, and he tries to find a solution to problems. The Invisible Clown is a scale that we aspire to.

Do you remember the incident with the cat meowing outside the door? Or, let's say you are on stage, and as if from nowhere a bird flies in through an open window, or a huge fly, or a cat jumps in. The public will see everything, and you too. A good performer would start to improvise: they leave the little bird alone and make them part of their performance. The meowing cat, the fly, and the bird represent an element of relativity and will embellish your performance.

On stage unforeseen events often happen. Ouspensky cites Gurdzhiev's words that he said to someone who had mistaken him for an oil magnate on a train:

*'It doesn't matter to us if there is a war or not
– we will always make a profit.'*[25]

RULE 8

**You are always in profit,
no matter what happens.**

Often we cannot change what happens to us, but we can change our attitude to what is happening around us. This is what it means to always be in profit.

To overcome our relativity — our fears, our desire to dominate, our greed, our striving to manipulate people, our self-will, our vanity — is to stop being a clown in the negative sense of the word. In order to release ourselves from these qualities we have to scale things up — we have to become an Invisible Clown.

RULE 9

Be the painting and not the artist.

Imagine that you are in an art gallery. You notice that next to each painting is the name of the creator of that piece, the artist, and everyone who visits the gallery is bothered by this question: 'Stop for a while, look at my painting. Do you like it?'

[25] Ouspensky, P.V. *In Search of the Miraculous*, SPB.: Izdatelstvo Chernysheva, 1992.

In their absurd behaviour this artist is acting more like a clown than an artist.

The same can be said of performance. You have created your work of art and you have rehearsed it. The time has now come to launch it. When we come into a museum, and we see a painting on a wall, we are interacting with this same painting, but the artist, however, is not standing next to it and is not asking whether we like their canvas or not — they created it, and now it lives it's own life. Visitors come and they look, sometimes they walk past this work without even glancing at it. The painting, in spite of this, continues to hang on the wall. It just EXISTS.

This is how I am with my performances: I take the artist out of it, leaving just the performance itself. This is what it means to send Mikhail Usov out into the auditorium.

THE SCALE OF POSSIBILITIES

You need to understand that a clown is not an idiot. That is to say, naturally they are idiots, and a good clown is always an intelligent idiot.

When you are on stage, stay one or two steps ahead of the public and prepare your new idea that you have to deliver ahead of time. That way a natural chain of bridges will appear for you, which will take you from topic to topic.

In order to create a single clowning act, I think of a whole clowning show. When I am creating a show, I am thinking about a whole clowning theatre, which could present lots of shows. Scale is an effective means of creating new material.

You can apply an idea of scale when you are working on any part of your performance, and then it will start to shine with the new aspects you have added.

I often hear from some directors: 'If you are already on stage, you have to give everything 100%.'

I want to argue the case with these directors. The striving to be better than you are gives rise to a chain of UNTRUTHS and may be bad for your physical health. The desire to perform some sort of a stunt is a manifestation of that same feminine dominance. To be who you are (where the key word is 'to be') on the other hand, gives rise to a series of TRUTHS, and to harmony. The public love harmony and will follow you even if you don't have the energy to give it 100%.

During a premiere of Cirque du Soleil in Amsterdam I broke my leg. I did not break it because I wanted to be better than I was then. There were a great many 'important people' at the show, the public really loved it, but I wanted to go beyond and to be funnier. I twisted a little out of nervousness and I broke my leg.

At Cirque du Soleil if you have pulled a muscle or if your spine is in pain and so on, a physiotherapist will ask you, in an attempt to understand if you can actually be allowed to work, to assess the pain in your spine on a scale from 1 to 10.

Let's use this wonderful scale and try to imagine that your psychological condition prior to a performance could be assessed only as a 5 on this scale. Do you have to perform at 10 on this scale? From my own experience with my broken leg I can conclude that: if you only have enough energy for a 5 today then you only have to perform at a five. If you only feel up to a 3 on this scale, then during the performance you should only aim for a three. Similarly, if you are very tired and your energy level is no more than 1, then perform at the same level, at a one.

If you make a good entrance, then your energy levels will increase and the level could go up to 10, that is to say, up to 100 percent. In that case you don't need to perform at eleven. If your energy does not go up to 10, however, don't worry: everything will be okay, just leave it at that. You always have to start with what you have. The public will definitely support you because you are not pretending to be anyone else, you are being who you are and you are the same as they are. The public will pick up on insincerity, histrionics, and hysterics immediately.

Another extreme: you are on stage and you feel like you are going to be successful on that day. The public are going to love you... Your emotions go off the scale, and the attention from the audience is like a narcotic. At that moment you relax under the influence of this narcotic, you blend in with the public, you lose your timing and your character, and you miss the moment, and as a result, you miss the next moment, and the next one.... and then you have to win the public's attention, and start all over again. For example, the audience give you an ovation, and you wait for 'two hours' for the clapping to die down. There are artistes who organize their performance in such a way that they rely on applause, they anticipate it, and, when the act is at an end and the auditorium have stopped clapping, the artiste does not leave the stage but asks again and again for applause, thinking that the public are fools. There have been so many occasions, however, when I have convinced myself of the opposite, the public are not fools. If you trust your Invisible Clown, you will not cling to fleeting success but you will continue to work for the greater good and, like the captain of a huge ship, you will bring your vessel to the port of destination, by-passing all dangers and challenges, and all moments of relativity that are dictated by your vanity.

There are many rules around how to perform, but if you follow all of them you could become very dry, or exceedingly intellectual, therefore being a performer should not detract you from being the person you really are.

In order to stop the flow of thoughts, you just have to say 'Stop!' in order to do this; however, you need to see this flow of thoughts. In order to be able to see this, there should be someone in us who is able to see it, and, once they have seen it, to say 'Stop!'

In the book 'The Dharma Bums' by Jack Kerouac, the hero recalls a piece of Zen-Buddhist wisdom:

'When you have scaled the heights,
keep on climbing.'[26]

This aphorism speaks to us of the need to expand our boundaries, our horizons.

In some instances it is useful to doubt things. It seems to us that we already know how to do something, but suddenly a completely new aspect of this same idea comes to light and it is perceived anew. The boundaries of knowledge and of ignorance have shifted.

Our intellect controls our emotions and our emotions control our intellect

If we are excessively emotional, we control our emotional state using our intellect; and we compensate for our excessive intellectuality using our emotions.

A mosaic in the Archiepiscopal Chapel in Ravenna, Italy depicts Christ as a warrior, and his right foot (the right side represents intellect) is standing on a lion — a symbol of our emotions, and his left foot (the left side represents our emotions) is standing on a snake, the symbol of intellect.

You should understand how to strike a balance between the character you have created and your timing. Do you remember how we have already researched the three forces on the journey to the Invisible Clown? Let's apply this principle here too. Therefore, there are three forces: an active force (which is a

[26] Kerouac J. 'The Dharma Bums,' – M.: Azbuka, 2013.

positive), a passive force (which is a negative), and a neutral force. The state of the Invisible Clown is always a neutral force, whilst timing and character can change. Sometimes you give priority to character, and this becomes an active force, or a positive. In this case timing becomes a passive force, or our negative. On another occasion you might focus on timing, and then this becomes an active force (a positive), and character transforms into a passive force (a negative). Only the Invisible Clown is able to discern what the public who have come to see the show on a given day are like, and what requires the greater attention at that moment — timing or character. Only the Invisible Clown knows what you need on a given day, so that either character or timing becomes an active or a passive force.

A permanent state for an artist is one of change — don't be afraid of change. Creativity is constant motion.

THE LESS YOU ARE, THE MORE YOU ARE

In reality there are very few modest people. I rarely meet such people. Crouching behind what we call modesty is a certain type of vanity, in the same way that consciousness stands behind true modesty.

The famous Canadian theatre and cinema director Robert Lepage is the most modest person. In the course of my career I have worked with a lot of directors, but Lepage is a special case. For instance, when he is producing his shows he does not use a microphone. After the final rehearsal of any part of his show, he is in no hurry to go on stage along with his production team, which consists of around ten people, including lighting designers, set designers, sound engineers, projectionists, set builders and so on, who always work with him on different projects in drama or opera theatres, circuses, and cinema.

Robert says little in a voice that is barely audible, but these ten people make note of what he says in their own way, and his secretary Madame Chalet writes everything Lepage says down in shorthand. At every one of his rehearsals the venue is completely silent. This is what he asks of every creative group he works with, from artistes to technicians.

The very first time I met Robert Lepage he told me that he did not like clowns. I was shocked by his admission, but later he said he did not like stupid clowns.

I have to admit I don't like them either and there is nothing worse than a stupid clown. After all, a clown is also an idiot. When a clown is a stupid idiot, though, they look like a psychiatric patient.

At our rehearsals with Robert there were always people around who were world famous. On one occasion, after another final rehearsal of my act, I approached the director with a new idea. Sitting next to him was an old man who looked no different from the people who were always around the director.

He said hello to me and said:

'Very funny.'

I answered:

'Thank you very much.'

Back stage they told me that it was Peter Gabriel.

Peter Gabriel is a musician, singer, and songwriter, my idol. I close all of my shows with his compositions. This was how I met my idol unexpectedly, not having recognized him.

Robert Lepage is a student of the great Peter Brook, the great Peter Gabriel's director — the most modest director I have ever met in my entire life. On one occasion, he was rehearsing Richard Wagner's 'The Nibelung's Ring' at the Metropolitan Opera in New York. He invited us as artistes of Cirque du Soleil to a general rehearsal. We sat in the balcony and below us in the stalls was Lepage, with his entire creative team.

After the rehearsal the usher approached me and asked me:

'Which of them is Robert Lepage, they have been rehearsing here for a week and we don't know what he looks like.'

I pointed out Robert to him.

'I never would have imagined that such a short person with so little that's attractive about him could be the great maestro Robert Lepage.'

It's true, Lepage is short in stature and a modest person, like the Invisible Clown.

I became friends with him not only because of what he represented for Cirque du Soleil, the show Totem, and more, but also for my clowning acts. Once I explained to him about my concept of the Invisible Clown. It turned out that he had also read *In Search of the Miraculou*s by Pyotr Ouspensky and even produced a play on that theme entitled 'The Geometry of the Miraculous.'

We became friends because of our spirituality, and it seems to me that this is the strongest sort of friendship.

Vanity, which I discussed at the start of the book, also has a bearing on our scale and relativity. Although to begin with it helps us to achieve results, introducing an element of competition, in the end it, like a worm, devours us from the inside out. As it grows into a cunning monster, sheltering behind our self-pity, our sense of guilt, pride, envy, jealousy, and greed, vanity saws away at our wings from the inside, so that as we are taking off we fall, imagining that we can fly.

It is impossible to get rid of this monster completely, the speed of its manifestation is so great that often all we do is catch hold of part of its tails, or we already find ourselves in a depression: suddenly we get frustrated with those around us, we close ourselves off to them, the world bears down on us, and we sense its injustice towards us. Some of us, the more active among us, try to influence the situation from the outside. We often look for solace in alcohol or in narcotics, which help for a short time, but after our hangover everything comes back to us and the monster of vanity gives rise to a feeling of guilt.

'And although our wins outweigh our losses, we nevertheless find ways to win.'

This was what the King of Hearts had once said.

And the poet Rumi wrote:

'This door, which is to be found in the present moment,
really is open.'

The main thing to be aware of when opening this door is our vanity. And although this warning looks very real, in fact it is an illusion, it is simply our shadow. It is absurd to be afraid of a shadow.

Vanity has a specific taste, and as soon as it begins to manifest, even in a harmless way, we should form the habit inside ourselves of going through the door into the present moment.

Let's say you greet someone and in response you hear: 'Give my regards to the stars!' You immediately feel a sense of pride because someone has called you a star. I can sense the taste of vanity in this. What would happen though if, as soon as you recognized it, you could open the door, not to pride, but to the present moment? You continue to talk to your interlocutor as usual, using your customary expressions and intonations, but what is more you suddenly hear your own voice, you see yourself and the person next to you — and all this through the present moment, through entering the state of the Invisible Clown. This state is a light, which no monster is able to overcome.

On social media I am often asked questions that relate directly to the topic of scale and relativity. Let's try and answer a few of them here.

I have experience working in small auditoriums for 150 people. How can you perform in a large hall in front of 2,000, or 5,000 people if you are not a rock musician?

It would be logical to think that in an enormous auditorium you have to work on a bigger scale: the amplitude of your movements needs to be greater, and your voice louder. I too thought this was the case for quite a long time, even more so when I worked in small theatres like the wonderful and famous Tigerplast Varieté Theater in Germany that holds 180 people. Then came Cirque du Soleil with 2,700 people, and then the legendary Royal Albert Hall in London that holds 5,000 people.

In large auditoriums I felt uncomfortable to begin with. I started to work on a bigger scale, and the organics of my performance were leaving me. On one occasion, however, as I was entering the state of the Invisible Clown, instead of becoming a larger figure on stage, I unexpectedly became a small dot. All my energy was concentrated on a small point in my tailbone. My character was enlivened and the public began to laugh.

Rule 10

You should become a small dot in a large auditorium.

This rule about becoming a small dot has helped me more than once. One of my clowning partners was very active. As he was always moving around quickly, all the public's attention was focused on him. I did not know what to do about this for a few months. That was before I heard the words of the King of Hearts:

"The less you are, the more you are.'

I had to stop moving completely, and also become very small on the inside, smaller than a microbe. To become a dot. A static dot.

The entire situation went through a 180-degree transformation. The audience were now looking at me. I became the main hero, and my partner — my theorist.

Where do you find the energy and strength when you are doing a lot of performances? Everyone needs energy, especially clowns: we are in front of the public every day and sometimes we have two or maybe three shows a day. Where do we find these reserves of energy? How do we avoid going on stage on autopilot given such an intense schedule?

Negative emotions, as well as superfluous conversations just prior to a performance, sap our energy that we need for our performance.

You have to remember that it is your body that is tired, and not you. You are not a body, but a drop, a part of the ocean, and you only need separate yourself from yourself, from your name, to separate your mug from the water inside it. Water never tires and it has no comprehension of tiredness, and water is older than the mug, it is eternal. You need to connect to that great flow. One of the ways you can find energy is to try as much as possible to be in the state of the Invisible Clown, and in the flow of the artistic creative process.

Creation is an inexhaustible source of energy. In order to draw something from it, however, you should not think of the result, because these considerations filter out the precious creative energy. After all, when we are creating we are at one with our Creator.

It is possible to have several creative projects going on at the same time. Right now I am involved with two shows and a couple of books.

Any activity, even the most mundane, like washing the dishes, can become creative if you don't just treat it as a necessary chore and bring an element of creativity into it.

We at the circus give around 360 shows a year, nine to ten shows a week. Even if your body is tired, and given the number of shows this is unavoidable, when you are in the present moment, in the 'here and now,' you discover an inexhaustible source of energy and your task is, at the right time, to chase away that thought that 'I'm tired.' If you are not able to chase away that thought in good time, however, it will creep into your head like a snake and will remain there for some time. Then you will need more, much more strength to drive it away.

How do the public differ in the various countries?

Many years ago, and even now, some clowns would go to street markets to get a sense of the tempo and rhythm of a location. I also do this sometimes and it really helps.

Each country has its own temperament. In countries like Austria, Switzerland, China, and Japan, we have to be very detailed in how we perform, we really have to spell out our performance. In England and Holland, however, audiences like minimalism, which means fewer colours and less movement.

In southern nations we have to perform more quickly and more passionately.

It is hard to reach the public, and yet at the same time it is easy. What we need to do is to be dressed in our costumes and at the same time be undressed. When this happens people will see that we are just like them. This is when we find our success.

LESSON 10 – HOW TO AWAKEN THE STATE OF THE INVISIBLE CLOWN IN THE VIEWER

The two remaining lessons are the most complex. They are even complex for me, because in order to write about the state of the Invisible Clown I have to experience that state for myself. That is to say, in order to share the state of the Invisible Clown with other people you have to be in that state yourself. Therefore, in the same way that bumblebees look for pollen in flowers so we will fly off today in search of the state of the Invisible Clown.

If the state of the Invisible Clown is very familiar to you already you don't need to look for a suitable location: you can experience this state at will anywhere you want to. For those of you who have no experience of immersing yourself in this state, I would advise you to go to the most beautiful location in your area.

The memory of this location will help you to awaken the state of the Invisible Clown and share this with your viewer.

The state of the Invisible Clown appears as a reaction to beauty and changes under the influence of beauty, because it is never static. I would suggest testing this assertion.

EXERCISE 11 ●

This time you will need to spend a little bit of money.

Buy an airline ticket to the American city of Las Vegas in the state of Nevada.

At Las Vegas airport hire a car and set off for the Grand Canyon in the state of Arizona. In three hours you will be there.

Park your car. Walk up to the edge of the canyon. You will have no need of me any more. Just look, listen. That is the state of the Invisible Clown. After about four seconds it will disappear because of the thoughts that will, like flies, come flying at you — so chase away any thoughts, even the most noble thoughts you have. Your task is to remain in this state whatever happens. Keep chasing away your thoughts and just remain the way you are at that moment.

What can you do though if you can't fly to Las Vegas? Find the most beautiful location in your town or in the countryside. If there is no such place then find the best patisserie shop where you live. Buy the tastiest pastry there and ask the sales assistant to wrap it up for you.

Find the most beautiful café where you live, where they brew the best coffee, or make the best tea. It is important not to save your money here. Going to this café is still cheaper than flying to the Grand Canyon in Arizona.

Find the best table and the best location in this café, and if that table is occupied wait for it to be free, even if you have to wait for a whole hour. Order a cup of coffee or tea. Now open your pastry and do this slowly, consciously, enjoy the state of the Invisible Clown.

As soon as this state appears don't be in any hurry to chase it away, it would be better to chase away your thoughts.

'To be, or not to be —
that is the question...'

These words by William Shakespeare are more pertinent here than in any other instance. When you ARE, and you know that you ARE — this is the greatest happiness. And when you are not present, when you are under the veil of imagination, of your thoughts, good or bad, then even the most beautiful place and the tastiest pastry have no meaning, because you ARE NOT PRESENT — and what cannot be cured must be endured.

When you need to go on stage or speak to your partners you will not forget about this experience. You will act on the basis of the state of the Invisible Clown, sharing this experience with other people.

CHAPTER 13

The Link Between The Invisible Clown and The Great Viewer

This chapter is about something that cannot be described in words, it cannot be seen with our two eyes, or heard, or touched. Nevertheless, let's try and encounter the Wonderful.

This Wonderful is remarkable because it is not subject to templates, and that means it is different for everyone. I will describe a few of my encounters with the wonderful, and in doing so, I will show you the way: how to look for and find the Wonderful for yourself.

THE IMPRESSION

In winter in the city of Dusseldorf it rains almost every day. The people here are clearly deficient in vitamin D. When they are able to immerse themselves in the state of the Invisible Clown, in those precious moments, they are no longer dependent on the sun's rays. This state in itself is the sun inside of us. It warms us, protects us, and brings us an inexplicable happiness.

In the turbulent nineties in the post-Soviet space there were a great many criminals. On one occasion I was on my way back from my latest tour around France and as was my habit I went into a café for a cup of coffee and to read my favourite book about Don Quixote.

At that time I was sitting in the café completely alone, and my reading awoke in me the state of the Invisible Clown. Suddenly, the door to the café opened and a group of bandits fell into the café; they had shaved heads and were dressed in sports gear.

It is surprising, but as I was in the state of the Invisible Clown this really didn't scare me.

The guys, there were six of them, sat at the table next to me. They were throwing looks in my direction. I just continued to read, experiencing an aesthetic pleasure from my book. Suddenly, one of the guys came up to me:

'Is that a good book?' he asked. He took the book from me. He read the title. He said:

'I am sorry.'

He gave me back my book, having opened it on the page I was on, and went back to the table next to me. These guys no longer paid any attention to me.

I continued to read, but I made a note to myself that the state of the Invisible Clown protects us from unpleasantness.

I often visit museums, and Rembrandt inspires me more than anything, his self-portraits and his portraits of other people. His eyes, his subjects' poses, as well as the blend of light and shadow, create a unique atmosphere. On one occasion I overheard a guide at the Hermitage. He was explaining that Rembrandt was an innovator. In order to gain volume and lustre he would mix ground glass into the paint. To illustrate soft light accurately Rembrandt would stretch a blank canvas, he would direct light onto it, and this light that reflected off the blank canvas he would use in his work. This approach is applied today in the film and photographic industries.

In the first chapter I explained how important it is to experience a moment of beauty: this is when the Invisible Clown manifests itself. What we read, eat, and what we look at — all this has a bearing on our connection with the Invisible Clown.

A human being can survive for up to two months without food if they have water.

Without air they can only survive for a few minutes.

A human being cannot live at all, however, without impressions. Imagine that you have no eyes, no ears, that you have no sense of smell, you have no sense of what you touch, no sense of objects, or of other people.

Impressions are also a food. It is important to choose the more refined impressions, especially when creating whatever it is that you do, your act or your show. Socializing with your friends is also a food for us.

You can gain pleasure from socializing and grow. Or on the contrary you can 'fall' too — for example, when a friend brings down your self-worth, or if it is difficult for you to say 'no,' or even to end the friendship altogether because of that feminine dominance. You, like a masochist, will put up with this attitude to you for your whole life.

Low-level impressions, when we are surrounded by dirt and squalor, can lead to depression, to a loss of your connectivity with your own life. Something similar happens to tramps and alcoholics and so on — their lives are full of low-level impressions and as a result these people fall even lower.

The higher the level of your impressions, the easier it is to reach the state of the Invisible Clown.

THE BLIND PEOPLE AT THE NOTRE-DAME CATHEDRAL IN PARIS

Once in Paris, I saw a surprising group of tourists: ten blind people came to visit the Notre-Dame Cathedral in Paris. The tour guide, who was pointing at the cathedral with his white stick, was also blind.

At first glance this was a completely absurd event.

Then I noticed that the blind people were touching a small model with their hands as they went into the cathedral. It seemed to me that we are more blinded than these blind people, even though we have our sight. Instead of seeing the cathedral for real and sensing it, all we do is take a selfie — me at the Notre-Dame in Paris. The photo is to say that we have been there — this is actually our entire vision and understanding of the cathedral.

If we could really see the Notre-Dame Cathedral in Paris, experience the unbelievable impression it makes on us, it is possible that we would not find any higher purpose within us to make a connection. When all we do is to take a selfie, all that happens is we find a connection with ourselves, our own cherished persona.

'Everyone needs gods.'

This phrase from 'The Odyssey' of Homer helps me in turn to understand our connection to the Divine. We need that connection even if we don't understand it. After all, without it we are like hens, we just live to eat, drink, and give birth to images of ourselves, and then end up in chicken soup.

As I was writing this chapter part of the Notre-Dame Cathedral in Paris burnt down, and now we have no chance of seeing it as it was. All we have are our 'me and Notre-Dame' selfies, but we only use these photographs to publish them on social media for some reason or other.

A FORETASTE OF THE DIVINE

In times past there were many more people who believed in God. It seems to me this is the reason why people are now suffering from depression: they have nothing to lean on.

We can try if only for one day, or for one hour, or five minutes of our lives, to trust the higher powers.

The only tool that we can use to connect with the Divine, or with the Great Viewer — is the Invisible Clown.

In the tenth chapter, I explained in theory a meeting between the Invisible Clown and the Great Viewer. Let's look at this meeting from a practical point of view.

I will just describe two incidents that happened to me so that you will have a better understanding of what I mean when I talk about a meeting with the Great Viewer.

You never know in advance what sort of a meeting will take place and when, so you always have to be prepared for it.

INCIDENT 1

I was going to work at the circus in The Hague on my bicycle. In this Dutch city there is an enormous number of bikes and almost everyone rides without a helmet. I had lots of time on my hands and I stopped a five-minute ride from the circus to drink a cup of coffee.

As I was leaving the café I decided not to put my helmet on as I only had a short distance to ride. As I was unhitching my bicycle the state of the Invisible Clown arose in me unexpectedly.

In this state I sat on my bicycle and I traveled just ten meters before a minibus in front of me stopped suddenly, went into reverse, and began to move straight towards me. I braked as hard as I could, unfortunately with the front brake, and I flew over the handlebars and the front wheel, and fell off my bicycle.

This happened very quickly. As I was in the state of the Invisible Clown, however, I can remember very clearly how I saw a white car, the yellowing leaves on the trees, the air, which I could have touched with my hands, how I braked, how long I was in the air, even though my flight lasted less than a second, and how I fell. For me this was a connection with the Great Viewer. The Great Viewer watched this spectacle.

I was lying on my stomach for a long time, not because I couldn't get up, but more because I was okay. Passers-by began to approach me and they wanted to help me.

'Don't help me people, please, I really am absolutely fine,' I thought. They helped me get to my feet and my wonderful state disappeared.

INCIDENT 2

The same epiphany happened to me in the French city of Clermont-Ferrand. When we were there on a tour I was trying as much as I could to be in the present moment. I noticed that whatever I was doing I would do by rote. I would even get out of bed in the morning always with the same leg. The moment when I went into the café, sat on the chair or got up from it, how I conversed with the people around me, how I formulated my thoughts, how my emotions appeared, and where they came from — all this came and went, but I was not present.

In this city of Clermont-Ferrand I decided to do everything consciously. The more I tried, however, the more clearly I noticed how I was not able to do anything consciously for a long period of time. Even the thoughts that came into my head that I could not do this gave rise to self-pity in me, and not consciousness.

When I understood that these were just thoughts, I had to leave them and continue to do these simple things, but now I would just do them consciously: to put on my left sock first, since I usually put the right one on first; to button up my shirt from the bottom to the top, as I usually buttoned it from top to bottom; to get up from a chair with my left foot, and so on.

I limited my reading of books and I would select music in such a way that I could listen to it on only one day, and at a certain time.

Two days went by in this vein; on the third day I left the hotel and set off for work at the theatre. It was a pleasant evening, a warm, light breeze was blowing, and the yellow light from the lamps was illuminating the street softly, like in Amsterdam. Suddenly, I understood that I was walking the same route as I had been the day before, my feet were leading me there. Then I turned into the street next to me and I realized that I did not have to walk: I could just stop. I stopped, and the whole world stopped for me: I sensed the state of the Invisible Clown.

'Look up' — I heard this thought clearly. This thought was familiar to me because in contrast to all my other thoughts, which came to me from somewhere unknown and went somewhere unknown, this was not a thought at all — this was MY OWN SELF, the one person who is never born, and never dies. (Don't try and understand this logically — you won't understand it). I looked up at a tree, an acacia tree, its leaves, like golden coins, twinkled in the yellow light. The twinkling of the leaves, like a hot knife through butter, cut a narrow trench to another dimension, the dimension of the Great Viewer. I understood that I had nowhere else to go. Standing in this location I realized that

I had come home. I understood that everything was surreal, the only real thing was the state that I was experiencing, and this is gifted to us not from our sight, or our hearing, or from our movements, or even from stopping our movements, and not from our thoughts, or our emotions. This was a familiar and indigenous feeling, as though I had come back home after a long journey. There was harmony in everything, and I was not thinking of changing anything at that moment at all.

When a thought came to me that I had to go to work it was hard for me to do this, as work also seemed surreal.

When I did reach the theatre and I opened the service door everything disappeared, like in 'Cinderella' by Charles Perrault.

The ball gown again turned into an old soiled dress, and the carriage with its horses and a coachman turned back into a pumpkin, mice, and a rat.

It is impossible to explain in words what I experienced at Clermont-Ferrand…

All we have to do is to consciously await our epiphany, our meeting with the Great Viewer and the Invisible Clown.

We need patience.

RULE 11

Don't interfere in your own fate.

This rule helps us to look at our own life as though it were a play, to not take it so seriously. When we are in a theatre or watching a film we are experiencing something, we worry about the heroes, and sometimes we can burst into tears.

We don't jump up onto the stage like Pinocchio or like Don Quixote, and we don't fight the puppet theatre. We know that it is just a play or a film.

Life is just such a film, in which we play our own role, and all that is required of me is to play this role consciously and not to interfere in my own fate.

To look at my life as if it were a play, which was written by an invisible screenwriter, one life puts before us a visible director.

AN ATMOSPHERE OF JOY

A tailor in Istanbul, a Sufi, told me two stories about vegetables.

A lot of vegetables were growing in a vegetable patch. In spring they looked like a green carpet with different patterns of flowers formed of different shapes and sizes. Bees would dance over the vegetable patch, as well as moths and small insects.

In the end one of the marrows grew to such a size that it blotted out the sun and there was no space for the other plants, as they had not stopped growing.

When he noticed this, the gardener picked the marrow and took it into the kitchen, for his evening meal.

The other story is about cucumbers and tomatoes that were growing on a vegetable patch. The vegetables were developing together. The flowers died away and the fruit appeared — small, green, and elongated cucumbers and small, round, and green tomatoes.

The vegetables smiled as they shone in the sun, and they reveled in the rain.

Time went by, however, and the tomatoes began to turn red. The cucumbers did not like this. They made an all out effort, trying to turn red as well but for all their efforts they only grew longer, and still stayed green. Then the longest cucumber said: 'How is that? How have the tomatoes dared to turn red? It so frustrating!'

The gardener intervened in this conflict of interests. He picked the cucumbers and the tomatoes. He sold some of them. He made a tomato and cucumber salad for his tea from the one cucumber that had complained the most.

Everyone has their own truth, but there is a higher level of justice.

For me these two stories are also a connection with the Divine. This connection is always there, even if we don't know it. In these two stories it is the gardener who acts as the Divine. The vegetables didn't even know he existed, and they ended up in a salad.

Is that not what happens in our own lives?

In order for the meeting between the Great Viewer and the Invisible Clown to take place, first you need to know how to experience the state of the Invisible Clown. To experience this state, however, the Clown has to gain strength. He grows up, and becomes strong and active BECAUSE OF Mikhail Usov. We have to strengthen our Clown, our inner child. To grow and develop the Clown needs special conditions, and first and foremost — a positive atmosphere.

When I began to work for Cirque du Soleil, I was surprised that we were always being praised. This experience was counter to the experience I had gained at the clowning studio in Russia, where we were shouted at almost every day. Here, when I knew that I had made a mistake I would be praised anyway. I would be told: 'You are amazing! The best!'

We were also banned from criticizing other artistes. A miracle happened before my eyes two years later, thanks to this positive atmosphere. The artistes who had joined Cirque du Soleil with me really did become the best at what they did.

Create a positive atmosphere around your creative work! Let a refusal to express negative emotions become a rule for you and for your team!

Value beauty! And then the Invisible Clown will throw himself into your arms.

Jalal ad-Din Rumi said:

'If you were self-sacrificial, your daily bread
would throw itself into your arms, the way lovers do.'[28]

An atmosphere of trust and positivity is important in anything you do.

Negativity can harm even the most successful of people. People lose their stimulus as a result of negative emotions and they grow tired and unsure of themselves. Positive thinking actually opens many closed doors and provides an opportunity for development.

Here is some advice that can help you to create a more positive atmosphere around you:

1. Take your partners and your co-creators and let them sense a moment of creativity — of creation.

There is nothing better than creativity. I have had the experience of working with several investors. I brought one of them into our creative process during the rehearsal of my

[28] Jalal ad-Din Rumi. Selected thoughts. http://www.omkara.ru/library/rumi2

show, inviting him to rehearse a small part of it as a director. He enjoyed creating something so much that he decided to invest additional money in this project. I remember another investor who, having recalled his prior experience, asked to become an actor and to act in a small scene in the film — and this was the result: he provided the money for an additional series.

2. Express your gratitude

By using that banal but absolutely necessary phrase 'THANK YOU,' we show our respect for another person, and we create a positive atmosphere.

3. Value the work of others

I somehow managed to create my own show and quite a few technicians began to work for me. Up until that point I had never presented any shows at all, I had only performed as a clown. I had no experience of working with people. I approached the technical services manager of our show, Mr. Canberra, for advice, in the hope that he would reveal some technical secrets to me.

Mr. Canberra said: 'You just need to remember one thing: each one of those technicians has a heart.'

This unbelievably simple practical advice helps lend something positive to the atmosphere around you, especially when you are creating something new and you are in a stressful situation.

4. Talk to people, make the first step to go and meet them.

Openness, even if it is not so pleasant, brings people together. When conflict happens the opportunity arises to become friends, so make the first move towards reconciliation.

5. Remember that we all see the world differently.

To understand your friends better, I would advise you to read the book 'Human Types' by Susan Zannos. In this book you will learn about the compatibility of different types of people, how they are attracted to one another, and how they are pushed away from one another. This information will allow you to choose partners much more effectively, and to manage your own business.

6. React the right way to criticism.

We should accept criticism addressed at us sensibly and steadfastly. We need to develop the right attitude to it. Often the most diverse motives are hiding behind criticism. Once, in New York, I opened a newspaper and was surprised at the negative reviews of our wonderful show; this included my own clowning acts. I asked our publicist why that newspaper had disliked us so much? He led me to the curtain, opened the edge just enough for the public to see, and said: 'This is why, because of a full auditorium, because of our success.'

The publicist explained that this publication, first and foremost, had been commissioned by one of the competing New York theatres.

7. Take small steps toward big goals.

Value the insignificant, almost unnoticeable steps. Small steps taken every day lead to success. I have tested this on my own show. We started from nothing, and every day we did something small. Two years later we had a wonderful show on our hands. Everyone knows that the enormous Apple Corporation started in a garage.

8. Try to see the amazing opportunities an individual has, and their potential for development.

I have already explained in this book how at Cirque du Soleil we — artistes, technicians, and office workers — are constantly being praised and treated with respect. This approach always bears fabulous fruit. Furthermore, socialize with people in such a way that they feel like they have already achieved the results you require of them.

The most consummate professionals are often born of the least self-assured and slightly intimidated individuals. If you see people as talentless, a poisonous atmosphere results, one of insecurity and fear. What can you create in that sort of atmosphere? Just monsters probably... I heard that in Silicon Valley in California they like unsuccessful people, those for whom a series of projects have ended in failure. At Google, employees who have experienced failure are valued for their experience. Those who have never made mistakes are seen as lacking experience. To make a mistake means you gain experience.

CHAPTER 14

The Choice is Yours

Our journey to the Invisible Clown is coming to an end,
now we are all Invisible Clowns. It's a paradox,
but the Invisible Clown — is only the start of the journey.
I would suggest not stopping, and setting off again on this path,
at the end of which you will all be Great Viewers.
I am sure that becoming a Great Viewer is not the end.
It is the start of a new journey, one that never ends.

OVERCOME YOUR INNER GIANTS

Everyone dreams of happiness and happiness itself is different for all of us. Someone might be dreaming of purchasing something they can afford, another person might want to sell something for the best price. Someone else might be thinking just about sweet dessert, another might be thinking about a politician who is not behaving as they should — instead of using the principle of 'divide and rule' in relation to themselves, they are dividing their people to rule over them, and they want their half of the world to join them. Someone might be dreaming of being healthy, of finding a new job, or of becoming famous. Someone is dreaming of watching the new film or of actually appearing in it, of winning a competition, of finding their other half they want to spend the rest of their lives with, or for just one evening. It seems to me, however, that this is NOT happiness. There are no reasons for happiness, and no conditions either. A response to this is hidden in the word happiness, it's the word 'NOW.'

In any set of circumstances, to be happy and satisfied we have to remain in the state of the Invisible Clown.

For instance, when we were told that due to coronavirus our circus would not be going to Rome or Milan or Prague and Rio de Janiero it meant that we would lose 12 months of work and around 360 shows. Believe me, when you have two small children, a bank loan on your house, and so on, news like that does not bring any particular joys at all.

As soon as you enter the state of the Invisible Clown, however, you become happy, because in a calm state of mind new opportunities open up.

In the uncertainty of our time, when we don't know what is going to happen tomorrow, we only have one way out — to live for today, for now.

You may remember that in this book I wrote about the endless variations, and the choices that we have before us. We can live according to a template of the mind, not able to sleep because of negative thoughts, which attack us just before dawn when we are completely unarmed. Either that, or we can calm our mind after seeing something wonderful, immerse ourselves in the state of the invisible Clown, and remain there. Then, that same mind conjures up a solution for us — a golden new idea.

My wonderful teacher the King of Hearts once said:

'The most dangerous virus in the world,
which kills billions of people — is the virus of imagination.'

In terms of imagination the King of Hearts is referring to a state in which an individual's attention is focused on what they don't have at that moment in time. In addition, he is referring to our false assumptions about ourselves, and our own capabilities. When our minds, like a veil, cover our eyes and make it difficult for us to see things clearly. This is how our imagination works as a negative factor.

In other words, our names that we carry inside of us, our Mikhail Usov, as they become active, throw up negative thoughts, which are gradually killing us. If we choose negativity and templates, and follow them, they will kill our body and we will start to get ill. The worst thing though is that our thoughts close off access to our soul.

'Timing — character — state' is just a method, which does not guarantee that you will be happy, it's merely a path that I am suggesting you take.

You may remember how, in an anecdote from Soviet times, a journalist asked Leonid Ilyich Brezhnev:

'Why do we have nothing to eat in the transition from developed socialism to communism?'

To which Brezhnev answered:

'We are on the road to communism, and nobody promised to feed us as we travel this road.'

Believe me, we are in a better situation, because as soon as we recall the state of the Invisible Clown and we immerse ourselves in it, we have nowhere else to go, our road is at an end.

Don Quixote, when he was traveling to the distant kingdom of Micomicon with his company to fight a giant, stopped at an inn. Don Quixote was so tired he fell asleep in the pantry, while his traveling companions were feasting in the public house. Suddenly, they heard shouting. This was Don Quixote battling the wineskins. When Sancho Pansa came running out to see what was happening, Don Quixote told him that there was no need to go and fight the giant in Micomicon any more, because he had fought him just then in the pantry, and he had won.

At first glance Don Quixote had been doing battle with the wineskins, but to me he had been fighting his own giants inside of him, his black wolf, his mug, his own name.

Giants, Goliaths, or our Mikhail Usov are always at the ready; at first glance they too are invisible, just like the Invisible Clown. In the same way, like the Invisible Clown, they are omnipresent and are at the ready, they differ from the Invisible Clown, however, in that they send us horrors, or the glories of yesterday, or of tomorrow.

These monsters cannot survive in the present, and we can use the present to subjugate them, exploit their energy, and direct it towards service. The choice is ours — we can either use this energy, or give in to it.

LESSON 11 — THE STORY OF YOUR LIFE

We have done a great deal of work and we have come to the final lesson.

This lesson is the simplest, and therefore it is the most complex. It reminds me of my trips around Egypt, particularly to the Great Pyramid of Giza.

In order to reach the Egyptian pyramids you need some considerable resources — money, time, and patience. The majority of the hotels are located in Cairo. You will need to look for a decent hotel, because in Egypt even the three-star hotels are not that good.

You will need a taxi to travel to Giza, as well as nerves of steel, because road transport in the country is chaotic.

To get inside the pyramids you need to get there early, because you will need to stand in long queues — firstly for the tickets, and then to get into the pyramid.

Standing in a queue in the desert under a roasting sun is not very pleasant.

But there you are, you have waited in the two queues, drunk almost two bottles of water, and at last you are heading into the pyramid.

You climb up a narrow staircase, all the way up to the top. It's stuffy and difficult to breathe. In the end you enter a sufficiently roomy pyramid that contains nothing, except a broken sarcophagus.

It is hard to escape the conclusion that there are no answers to be found in the external world. No matter how hard we tried to find the secrets of those same pyramids, no matter how many new rooms we might find in the pyramid, our minds would just come up with new questions. The answer is not in what we can see with our own two eyes, but in what we can't see with them. What we are trying to find — is our internal factor, and not our external one.

EXERCISE 12 ●▬▬▬▬▬▬▬▬▬▬▬▬▬▬▬▬▬▬▬▬

This time you will need a sharpened pencil and an eraser.

It is time to enjoy the fruits of your work on yourself. You will not need me any more. From here on it's your own experience. Start by being like Adam, the first human on Earth, from a clean slate, and do what you think is necessary.

The next page is empty.

Now it's your turn: avoiding templates, use this space to start to write the story of your life. Every day you will encounter a choice you have to make, to live according to templates or not. If you see templates again, it would be better to erase what you have written and leave the page blank.

The Story of Your Life

The Story of Your Life

AFTERWORD

At the beginning of the 2000s I moved to Germany. To begin with, the issue of money became very acute. I had enough reserves for no more than three months. Despite the fact that by that time I had two reasonable clowning acts, I could not find work anywhere.

It was unbelievably difficult to break into the circus market in Germany, and in Europe. Even recording a video was difficult because I needed a live audience in a variety show or at a circus. I was prepared to perform for free in exchange for recording a video. Any show would work for this.

Unfortunately, however, nobody wanted to invite me to perform, even for free. More often than not the directors of the circus or theatre explained their rejection by saying that they already had a whole show, and that I would look out of place there with my acts.

My money was dwindling and I was forced to go and perform on the street. In Germany, in order to perform on the street you need to go to the police and pay 10 Euros, and get a permit from them.

At that time I did not have any experience of performing on the street. It seemed like this was another world. One that was completely different to the circus or a theatre. A street clown should react to everything, whatever happens to the passers-by, vehicles, animals, or objects, such as a plastic bag carried on the wind. A clown should be a good improviser. That's not all though. A street clown should organize their space in such a way that they are able to make a stage out of a small area, a grey, boring asphalt, and the everyday passers-by, the onlookers, are transformed into their public, and they become their clown, their artiste.

The earnings of a street artiste depend on this.

I, however, did not yet know these rules, or understand them. Having paid for my permit at the police station I applied my make up, took my small tape recorder with speakers, and my clowning costume, and headed for the church of Saint Laurence in Nuremberg.

I set up next to a window in the 'Karstadt' shopping center. I put my hat out in front of me and then, to get things started, I put one Euro into the hat myself. I turned my music on. I then began to perform. I had no idea who I was performing for, as the pedestrians just walked past... No, they looked at me attentively, but nobody stopped, and what is more, nobody threw any money into the hat.

My clowning act came to an end, but all that was in the hat was still that one coin that I had thrown there myself.

I took a five-minute break, I drank some water, put the hat straight, switched on some music and performed a second time, repeating the same act, with the self same effect. Nobody thanked me in any way at all.

I packed up my things and, crushed by this failure, I went home.

A street show is not for me, I thought to myself.

The following day this story had its continuation.

In the morning I had to go to the arbeitsamt, or the employment agency. I had to explain why I was not working, and I also had to register so that they could find me some mundane temporary work — maybe they could offer me street cleaning or fruit picking.

A tall and beautiful woman met me at the entrance to the office, and offered me a seat. She asked me about my profession, and I answered, saying I was a professional clown. She looked straight at me, and asked if it had been me the day before next to the 'Karstadt' shopping center juggling ping-pong balls. I had to admit it had been me. She said she had walked past me the day before as I had been performing.

This woman then began to print something off that seemed to take a long time.

Then she told me that I was a real professional clown and that it would be wrong to turn me into an unskilled worker. So she asked me to bring her video recordings of my acts, and she promised that the agency would help me to sell my acts on the German market. She also said that while I was waiting for work as a clown I would receive an unemployment benefit and medical insurance.

The sense of joy that I felt is hard to describe. I got my first assignment in a German variety show after seven months. All this time, however, I could rehearse without worrying about money, I could rent some premises to record videos of my acts, and send these videos to theatres around Europe.

Even though nobody had dropped a cent into my hat next to the 'Karstadt' shopping center, in actual fact in those fifteen minutes of 'street clowning' I earned myself seven months of living in Germany.

There is a sense in everything that happens to us, there are always reasons, and consequences. We, however, don't see the whole picture. We worry so easily and we are often disappointed over a cent, over the small details.

I recall another funny story that my friend, who is a millionaire from Odessa, told me. He once came to Germany. When you buy bottled water in a shop in Germany, the cost includes 20 cents for the plastic bottle, and the local inhabitants do not throw the bottles away, they collect them and give them back to the shops (incidentally this is why you don't see plastic bottles discarded on the street in Germany).

My friend went to buy some provisions and at the same time he decided to return his empty bottles that he had collected at home. One of the bottles was non-standard, and he had more than likely brought this bottle over from the Ukraine. Naturally, the German girl who worked at the till did not want to accept this bottle. My friend started a huge argument in the shop and they called the manager. The fastidious Germans apologized to him but they still did not accept the bottle.

Suddenly, our millionaire admitted right there, in the shop, that he was a millionaire. What need did he have of this bottle? Without saying a word he chose three bars of chocolate, bought them, and gifted them to the people he had been arguing with a moment before.

We want to fight in our little corner. It seems to me that we worry over the small things because we experience a lack of TRUST. We don't trust our own fate, and we don't have faith in the higher powers. Trust is a topic that inspires me. Not faith, but specifically *trust*.

When we can't see our connection to the Divine, we need faith. When we encounter the Divine, we need trust.

A long time ago in Paris, I watched a puppet show by Philippe Genti. I could suddenly see the strings the miniature puppet Pierrot was attached to. These strings connected him to Philippe Genti. The puppeteer manipulated Pierrot using these strings. The puppet wanted to stop being a puppet once they had seen that they were suspended on strings. Genti cut off the strings. Without these strings he cannot stand up. The puppet fell down and the puppeteer picked up the lifeless body of Peirrot very gently and touchingly, and took him behind the scenes at arms length.

We are also puppets and we are also being moved around on the end of invisible strings. We also have to cast off a lot of the strings we no longer need. The strings of vanity, pride, and fear, leaving just some in place so we don't lose our connection to the Divine.

At the beginning of the 1920s Stanislavskiy, in response to a question from one of his students on what the ideal theatre should be like, answered:

> *'If there could be such a thing as the ideal theatre, then*
> *it should probably be a theatre that has these qualities: one that*
> *is on a higher plane, and is easier, simpler, and more joyful.'*[29]

It seems to me that these words could relate to an act, a show, an image, and to our own lives.

Recently Stanislavskiy appeared to me in a dream.

The fear that he would now say, 'I don't believe you,' had gone, but the wish that he would say, 'I believe,' was not there either.

Konstantin Sergeyevich looked at me, smiled, and said very softly:

'I TRUST YOU.'

---

[29] From Anatoliy Smelyanskiy's own show, dedicated to K. Stanislavski's 150th birthday. The television channel 'Kultura,' 2013. https://www.youtube.com/watch?v+64mHhhzKQ1A.

ACKNOWLEDGMENTS

I want to express my gratitude to the people without whom this book would have not have seen the light of day. My wonderful parents, who truly gave me freedom of choice when they let me, as a 16-year-old, travel from Kharkov to distant Kazakhstan. This played a decisive role in my choice of profession, and in my journey in life.

To my brother, Vitaliy Usov, for his endless patience.

To my first circus teacher, Verteim Moiseyevich Savelie, who turned my life around.

To my dear friend and my first clowning partner, Armen Vladimirovich Asiryanets, for his endless good humour and nobility.

To my dear friend and gentle clown, Mik, Nikolai Kormiltsev, for his spiritual searches.

To the wonderful clown and mentor, Vladimir Ivanovich Kremene, for his trust in me.

To the wonderful and legendary director of all clowns, Vladimir Konstantinovich Kryukov, who first recognized the soul of a clown in me.

To the wonderful Director, Tereza Gannibalovna Durovoy, who believed in me and afforded every opportunity to experiment in her own theatre.

To the wonderful Director, Aleksandr Anatolyevich Makarov, thanks to whom, I fell in love with the absurd and with alogism.

To the wonderful director and Clown, Klepe, Vitaliy Alekseyevich Dovgan, who taught me patience and the value of hard work.

To my friend and clowning partner, the wonderful White Clown, Nikolai Bereza, for his relaxed and good nature.

To my friend and clowning partner, the wonderful Clown Paganel, Sergey Davydov, for his kindness of heart.

To my friend and clowning partner, the wonderful Clown Kotini Junior, Konstantin Andreychenko, for his unwavering devotion to a creative approach.

To my friend, the Poet Artur Sukurkin, for his generosity of spirit.

To my dear friend the Director, Anatoliy Zalevskiy, for his absolutism, and his enormous optimism.

To my dear teacher and Director, Robert Lepage, for his trust in me.

To the wonderful Clown, Slava Polunin, who, without studying it, taught me silence.

To my friend the wonderful director from Leipzig, Urs Jaeckle, for his constant support in my creative work.

To my wonderful Director and the Founder of the Tigerplast Theatre in Frankfurt-am-Maine, Margareta Dillinger, for constancy, trust, and love for art.

To my wonderful producer, the Director Natasha Gamolskaya-Radzinskaya, for her great creative breakthroughs and her inspiration.

To my wonderful friend, the producer and investor Antonio Boksieri, for his good nature and his generosity of spirit.

To the unbelievable prima ballerina of the Bolshoi Theatre, Mariya Aleksandrova, for her participation in greatness.

To the co-founder of the online school of writing, GetPublishED, and to the Deputy Editor-in-Chief of the publishing house 'Alpina Publishing,' Irina Gusinskaya, who taught me how to write books.

To my friend, the clown Igor Mamlenkov, for his help in creating this book.

To my friend Margaret Jean Campbell, for her generosity, and for teaching me to achieve the goals I have set for myself.

To my dear friend and Teacher, Robert Earl Burton, for inviting me into the PRESENT.

And the biggest thanks go to my wonderful family, to my children, and to my wife Olga Usova, for her angelic patience, and for her trust and her love.

P.S. Today students often send me short videos with their rehearsals and performances so that I can edit them, or I can provide commentary, or give advice. Therefore, I have decided to create an online school for those who want to learn about performing in public, develop their charisma, and overcome the fear of being on stage.

If you have enjoyed my book, I would be delighted to see you in my online courses and workshops at Inside-Theatre. com

BIBLIOGRAPHY

Burton R. *Self-Remembering*– M.: IG 'Ves,' 2011.

Burton R. *Awakening*. Robert Burton's Quotes / edited by D. Crossby. – M.: IG 'Ves,' 2011.

Cervantes M. de. *The Ingenious Don Quixote of La Mancha*. – M.: AST, 2003.

Collin R. *The Mirror of Light*. – SPb.: The Chernyshev Publishing House, 1997.

Collin R. *The Theory of Celestial Influence*. – SPb. The Chernyshev Publishing House, 1997.

Eckermann, I.P. *Conversations with Goethe*. – M.: RIPOL classic, 2020.

Khayyam, O. *The Rubaiyat*. – M.: Eksmo, 2019.

Kukarkin A. *Charlie Chaplin*. – M.: Iskusstvo, 1988.

Rumi D. *Treasures of Recollection*. – M.: Realityweb, 2010.

Stanislavski K. *I Don't Believe you!* Memoirs. – M.: AST, 2015.

Stanislavski K. *An Actor's Work on Themselves*. – M.: Eksmo, 2017.

The Encyclopedia of the Circus and the Performing Arts on the website: http://www.ruscircus.ru/.

The New Acropilis. URL: https://www.newacropilis.ru/.

Ouspensky P. *In Search of the Miraculous*.– M.: The Chernyshev Publishing House, 1992.

Whitman W. *Leaves of Grass*. – M.: Azbuka, 2019.

Yengibarov L. *The Final Round*. – Yerevan.: Sovetakan grokh, 1984.

Zannos S. *Human Types. Building Your Body and Your Psychology*. – M.: IG 'Ves,' 2003.

The Invisible Clown